Jon + b

MW00937044

Thank you for letting us stay
in your home! Whitney + I
feel rested and encouraged after
our trip.

I hope you enjoyer the book
and that your hearts our
stirred toward our Lord

Faithful is He,

~ Charles

Let the redeemed of the Lord
say so ~ Ps 107

A PECULIAR JOURNEY

Understanding Joy in Suffering
on the Road to Huruma

Charles J. Prichard

WESTBOW
PRESS®
A DIVISION OF THOMAS NELSON
& ZONDERVAN

Scripture taken from the New King James Version®. Copyright ©
1982 by Thomas Nelson. Used by permission. All rights reserved.

WestBow Press books may be ordered through booksellers or by contacting:

WestBow Press
A Division of Thomas Nelson & Zondervan
1663 Liberty Drive
Bloomington, IN 47403
www.westbowpress.com
1 (866) 928-1240

ISBN: 978-1-9736-3522-2 (sc)
ISBN: 978-1-9736-3523-9 (e)

Library of Congress Control Number: 2018908815

Print information available on the last page.

WestBow Press rev. date: 8/8/2018

PRAISE FOR A PECULIAR JOURNEY

Each chapter leads you deeper into the Scriptures probing the elements of a full walk with Christ…It will lead you into significant self-examination.

Jerry E. White, PhD
Major General, USAF Retired
International President Emeritus, The Navigators

Charles encountered the deep suffering of the residents in Huruma Village and allowed it to take him to a deeper encounter with The One who alone can help us make sense of our suffering. Jesus Christ died to restore the hope that the sin of the world viciously destroys. Let us preach this good news.

Irene Tongoi
Founder, New Dawn Education Centre, Kenya

Powerfully inspiring and theologically rich! Charles brings to light the reality of suffering and the real-world, practical applications to understanding and overcoming hardships through resilience and hope.

Robert F. Dees
Major General, USAF Retired
President, Resilience Consulting

God-centered, Christ-exalting, Scripture-saturated, Spirit-led. Therefore, this book is extremely practical on how to live out the normal, yet supernatural Christian life. Charles is a faithful brother who wears many hats well. I pray that this book will lead many pastors and church members to pray more fervently and sacrifice more willingly that God will use their daily lives for His glory and the joy of all people in Christ. To live is Christ!

Tom Clemons
Senior Pastor, Monument Hill Church, CO

A Peculiar Journey is an impassioned consideration of the role of suffering and sorrow in the life of the believer. Prichard provides a clear survey of what Scripture teaches in regards to tragedies we face. We cannot be reminded enough that embracing difficulty, rather than fleeing from it, is the path which God intends us to walk; and that it is all for our good and His glory.

Ben Zornes
Author/Musician

The words and thoughts throughout this book are truly a work of art and will be blessed by God. It is very refreshing to see how *A Peculiar Journey* captivates the reader with its candid comments and biblically supported insights. Each chapter makes you look inwardly upon what we can or cannot accomplish, but even more so upwardly at what God has done and continues to do for us sinners. We as Christians have such an advantage over the world as we have the knowledge of where we get to spend eternity—happily, heaven bound—but not until the Lord says so. I pray that this book will reach the masses and make revolutionary changes to mankind's warped worldly view while making people want to start that needed relationship with Jesus—our Savior for all time!

Timothy Woller
President, Saba International

Charles provides a great Biblical perspective, a global story, and practical ideas to help us stay wise and keep trusting God in the midst of suffering which is one of the main ways God uses to grow our faith in Him.

Jim Lee
Deputy Director of Air Force Ministries, The Navigators

You don't have to be a victim of suffering to learn from it, but you must have a heart of compassion to become aware of the suffering that surrounds us. A Peculiar Journey helps us "walk" through suffering with Biblical truth, real life testimonies, and challenging questions to meditate on.

Felix Colonnieves
Another follower of Christ

To my brothers and sisters from Huruma Village, Kenya.
Thank you for your joy and love for Jesus Christ. I
pray that you will follow Him all the way home.

Asante Sana. Nakupenda![1]

---

[1] "Thank you very much. I love you!" in Kiswahili (Kenyan Swahili)

CONTENTS

❖❖❖

ACKNOWLEDGEMENTS

This book is the fruit of God's perfect grace, which has been given to me through Jesus Christ. I am grateful to Him for saving me from my sins and making me His. I also thank Him for giving me the desire to want to love and continually know Him more. All of this work is for Him (1 Corinthians 10:31) and my prayer is that all will see His unfathomable grace toward me and thereby witness His wondrous glory (John 3:30). This book is ultimately for the One apart from whom I can do nothing (John 15:5).

I am thankful for my beautiful wife and best friend, Whitney, for her love and encouragement as I slowly wrote this book over a period of three years. Of all husbands on earth, I feel the most indebted. I want you to know that I love you, and thank God for you every day.

Thank you also to Sam Whatley, Suzi Park, and Buzzie Gray for the time they took to carefully edit my manuscript. They truly have incredible gifts of writing, and their meticulous comments and suggestions helped make this project possible.

I am indebted to my brothers and sisters in Huruma Village, Kenya who first shared their stories with me in 2011, and continue to inspire me and the world with their genuine love for Jesus and His people. Thank you for your hospitality, for treating me as your own, and teaching me so much about the reality of experiencing joy amidst suffering. I know that even personal, handwritten letters are not enough and so I long to see you face to face again, so that I may encourage you in your walk with Jesus (Romans 1:11, 2 John 12, 3 John 13-14).

In Him,
Charles Prichard "Shujaa"[2]
Psalm 71:18

---

[2] Shujaa means warrior or soldier in Kiswahili. I was given this name by the young men in Huruma Village, Kenya. They thought it was fitting because Charles means "warrior" in old English and they called me soldier when they found out that I was in the U.S. Military.

FOREWORD

⟡ ⟡ ⟡

I know suffering. At least I know *my* suffering. Our 30-year-old son was brutally murdered on his job. And we suffered. But in the midst of the reality of loss, I was driven to my knees, to the Word, to friends, and certainly to God. Yet we know so many who are driven away from God into bitterness and resentment. Suffering is only one of the life experiences that drive us to discover God in a deeper way. More importantly, it is something totally out of our control. We suddenly realize that what we thought gave us joy and satisfaction had little meaning. In my case, being President of The Navigators and an Air Force general suddenly lost their luster. The deeper realities of life and of God dug deeply into my soul. What now?

In *A Peculiar Journey*, the "What now?" becomes the central theme of walking with God in the midst of real life. Charles digs into the Scriptures to guide us into the life of true discipleship and practical commitment. Before suffering one would be tempted to say, "Oh, I know that." After suffering or in the midst of suffering the response is "I really need to learn and understand this." The theme of hope and joy emerges from the bed of suffering, whether small or large. This hope and joy that we all want grows out of this deep knowledge of God and His Word applied to the reality of life. This is not just theory or theological musings. This is where the rubber meets the road in testing whether or not our faith is real.

Each chapter leads you deeper into the Scriptures probing the elements of a full walk with Christ. Gone are the simplistic ideas of just receiving salvation in Jesus and all will be well. It will lead you into significant self-examination. Peter crystalizes the goal: "In this you greatly rejoice, though now for a little while, if need be, you have been grieved by various trials, that the genuineness of your faith, being much more precious than gold that perishes, though it is tested by fire, may be found to praise, honor, and glory at the revelation of Jesus Christ" (1 Peter 1:6-7).

I don't like the fire. But I am so much the better for it.

Jerry E. White, PhD
Major General, USAF Retired
International President Emeritus, The Navigators

PREFACE

❖ ❖ ❖

I know for a fact that if the words in this book cause even one reader to seek the Lord Jesus Christ, it will not have been written in vain.

Upon my return from a mission's trip in Africa, I developed a broader and deeper understanding regarding the theology of suffering and poverty alleviation. At the same time, I had a burning desire to articulate to a lost world how suffering is never beyond God. I wanted to be able to point others to the One who alone, is able to make sense of the hardships we experience in a fallen world. After seeing a group of people experience extreme suffering and still retain their joy, I was eager to dig deeper and figure out how that was even possible.

As my research on this topic progressed, I began to realize that Scripture confirmed what I saw in a slum in Kenya. Those who are connected to Him can truly find meaning and comfort in their life regardless of their circumstances. The apostle Paul said that Christians can, "glory in [our] tribulations"

(Romans 5:3) and James urges us to "Count it all joy when [we] fall into various trials" (James 1:2a). I had memorized these two verses when I was a younger and have come to understand them in a deeper and greater light.

I pray that you will read this book and come away with a deeper encouragement to study God's Word more. I implore you to have a Bible in your hand, and look up the Scripture references in the end notes of each page as you read this book. I know that many of the concepts in this book will be difficult to comprehend or understand if you do not take time to reflect, which is why I included some questions for you to answer at the end of each chapter, along with a short testimony relating to the chapter. Although the names are changed to protect the privacy of each individual, the stories are true. I know that you will find them inspiring.

For the untold numbers of people passing through extreme sufferings, understanding the biblical teachings on suffering will be enlightening as you strive to "make sense" of what you are experiencing or have experienced in the past. Finally, for those who are living a life of comfort and affluence, this book may serve as a wakeup call as you are constantly tempted to rely on and find happiness in the temporary and fleeting pleasures of this world.

Suffering is real. True joy is possible. May God grant you wisdom as you seek the Truth.

INTRODUCTION

❖ ❖ ❖

Many view the story of Job in the Bible as fictional and fail to realize that there are brothers and sisters around the world who suffer, and yet still experience joy. While in the Kenyan village of Mji wa Huruma in 2011, I developed an appreciation for the mundane that seemed to overshadow the daily hardships of the villagers.

The village of Huruma is situated in the Karua Forest and borders the wealthy neighborhood of Runda. The conditions of the slum are inhumane. The homes are built from rusted sheet metal that form a close cluster, and house approximately five thousand villagers within two square miles. The pervasive stench of both human and animal excrements viciously assaulted my senses as I was given a "village tour," and seemed to saturate every fiber of cloth that covered the bodies of the villagers. While walking through the rain that day, I struggled to keep my balance navigating between houses as the slippery dark, reddish-brown mud (or what I trusted was mud) stuck to the soles of my shoes. When I first entered the village, my eyes took in the tranquil sight of a community of people cultivating the small land they possessed. After being escorted through the village by two young Kenyans, my attention turned to Mutua.

Mutua was nineteen when I first met him. His quiet, yet authoritative demeanor struck me as we shared our respective testimonies of God's provision in our lives. For the first week, when most of my conversations with this young Kenyan ended, I was left entranced with the ambiance of the pure joy in his life. I later came to realize that his inner happiness and peace did not stem from his circumstances. His mother had abruptly died from illness ten days prior to our initial conversation. Suddenly orphaned, Mutua had taken full responsibility as the sole provider for his siblings and a few of his younger cousins. While many nineteen-year-olds in Western cultures still choose to act like boys, this young Kenyan demonstrated leadership and set an example of nobility in his village. With a sustained passion for the wellbeing of his family, Mutua chose to have an elevated perspective on suffering, which could very well change an entire community and culture.

A prime example of this, is how Mutua never complained or asked for money while I was with him. He rarely spoke of his hardships but instead, focused his discussion on encouraging me to seek contentment and godliness in life. Whenever I asked him how he was doing, he would promptly respond with, *Bwana Asifiwe*, which means, "Praise the Lord" in Kiswahili.

I spent the majority of my time in Huruma surrounding myself with the young men in the village. The longer I stayed, the more I developed relationships with others who were high-school (or what is known in Eastern Africa as secondary school) aged. After hearing his story years later, one individual caught my attention for a number of reasons. Abused by his drunkard father, Hodari and his seven siblings were also abandoned by their mother. This forced their widowed grandmother to raise them in severe poverty. As a twenty-one-year-old at the time, I couldn't imagine taking on that weighty responsibility.

How can one be content and joyful amidst dire circumstances? How can one be at peace when everything is taken from him? After leaving Huruma Village, I was convinced beyond doubt that the apostle Paul's letter to the church in Rome was divinely inspired. He told them that they could rejoice in their suffering. Why? Because it produces perseverance, character, and hope (see Romans 5:3-5). What is this hope? This hope does not disappoint, and for Mutua, his is a testimony of eternal hope. Portions of this book are stories of a group of people who continue to demonstrate resilience as they overcome incredible physical, mental, emotional, and spiritual challenges. This is the story of a group of people who have shown the world how real joy can be experienced amidst suffering.

CHAPTER 1

What is Suffering?

And not only that, but we also glory in tribulations, knowing that tribulation produces perseverance; and perseverance, character; and character, hope. Now hope does not disappoint, because the love of God has been poured out in our hearts by the Holy Spirit who was given to us.

—Romans 5:3-5

Character cannot be developed in ease and quiet. Only through experience of trial and suffering can the soul be strengthened, ambition inspired, and success achieved.

—Helen Keller

Origin of Suffering

Suffering is not a created thing. While cold is the absence of heat and darkness is the absence of light, evil is the absence of good. More specifically, evil is the absence of God. While God did not create evil, sin, or suffering, He did allow for the possibility of them to exist. Had He created humans without the will to choose, they would all be robots where instead of mankind electing to serve God out of love and adoration, they would serve Him out of obligation.

We know from recorded history that in the beginning, God created the universe. He spoke it into existence. After six days of creation, He declared that everything was good. He created the first man (Adam) and the first woman (Eve) in the likeness and image of Himself. Mankind was distinct from the rest of creation. Humans were given a conscience and the ability to choose right from wrong. Before sin entered the world, suffering was absent. Suffering came about as the consequence of sin and evil. Prior to that, Adam and Eve dwelt in the garden of Eden with God in perfect shalom.[3] As a result of sin however, God's relationship with mankind was shattered when our first father and mother chose to deny His goodness. Before sin entered the world,

---

[3] Shalom is a Hebrew word meaning perfect peace, harmony, completeness, prosperity, and wholeness.

mankind did not experience or understand any form of suffering. God created the world and called it good. Through mankind's rebellion, sin fractured that goodness which allowed suffering to flourish.

Despite sin, God still uses suffering for greater purposes. The historical account of Joseph clearly demonstrates God's sovereignty over suffering, as Joseph said to his brothers who sold him into slavery because of their jealous and envious hearts, "you meant evil against me, but God meant it [used it] for good" (Genesis 50:20). Despite the brothers' sinful ways, God used suffering and hardship to rescue His people by bringing them out of a severe famine and into the land of Egypt.

Suffering Defined

The term suffering is derived from the Greek word *pathēma* which means an enduring affliction or hardship. This word is used in the Scriptures to describe both outward sufferings (physical) and inward sufferings (emotional, psychological, and spiritual). Although the word itself is not outstanding, it takes on extraordinary meaning within the context of God's Word.

Before we look at specific instances where *pathēma* is used, let us first examine the apostle Paul who frequently spoke and wrote about the subject in his thirteen epistles (letters), which are some of the most famous writings recorded in human history.[4] Paul (originally named Saul), along with his father, was a Pharisee and Roman citizen.[5] He was a descendent in the line of Benjamin with Hebrew ancestry, and was born in Tarsus in Celicia, a province which is now Turkey.[6] Paul went out to study under a renowned rabbi named Gamaliel, and mastered Jewish history and law through the careful examination of the Torah, psalms, and prophets. Paul also learned to articulate, debate, and enforce every detail that was laid out in Jewish law through Moses and the prophets.[7] With this zeal for the Jewish law, he spent his early adult life persecuting the Christian church after Jesus' resurrection due to his zealousness for the law.[8] However, Paul's life changed on the road to Damascus when he surrendered his life to Christ after his heart was changed and eyes were opened to his desperate need for Christ's mercy and forgiveness.[9]

---

[4] Almost four billion copies of the bible (and Paul's writings make up a third of the New Testament) were printed and sold globally in the last five decades. Read more at www.relevantmagazine.com/slices/bible-tops-list-most-read-books-world

[5] Acts 23:6, 22:25-28

[6] Acts 22:3

[7] See Acts 25-28

[8] See Acts 7:59, 8:1; Philippians 3:3-7

[9] Acts 9:3-19

Paul's life is a remarkable example of God's grace as sinful, broken individuals are transformed every day with the knowledge of salvation through Jesus Christ. When we read the history of Paul, we see that no one—not even the "chief of sinners" (1 Timothy 1:12-17)—is too far from God's love. If God can reach the hardened heart of a wicked man named Saul, He surely can save anyone who is willing to humbly repent and believe in Him.[10]

In the eighth chapter of his letter to the church in Rome, Paul uses the word *pathēma* twice. In verse 17, he says that Christians are glorified with Christ *if* we suffer with Him. We see that this glorification in Jesus is a future glory that we receive when He takes us home (heaven) as an inheritance that will never perish.[11] This inheritance was bought at a price (by Jesus' death on the cross), which is why Paul also urges fellow believers to honor God with their bodies.[12] Similarly, in Romans 8:18, Paul says that the suffering of this present time should not even be compared to the glory of being with Christ in eternity. In the end, Paul sees (and experiences) suffering as a temporary reality of life that can be overcome by the hope that we have in Christ.[13]

---

[10] Romans 10:9-10

[11] 1 Peter 1:3-6

[12] 1 Corinthians 6:20

[13] Romans 8:23-29

Indeed, Paul understood the purposes of suffering and as a result spoke with authority on the matter, as his life was far from easy. Over a period of a few years, he was whipped (near to death) a total of 195 times on five separate occasions. Additionally, he was beaten with rods, stoned, shipwrecked, and imprisoned in some of the harshest prisons.[14] Yet in all these things, he was able to overcome by the consolation of knowing that these hardships were brief, compared to the eternal glory that he would receive when God would take him home.[15]

In his second letter to Timothy, Paul said that he was not ashamed of his sufferings because he knew Christ.[16] In other words, Paul saw Christ as superior to the fleeting pleasures and hardships of the world. He saw his sufferings as a way to know Christ more. God used his sufferings to help Paul understand that all he had was counted as a loss—all except the glory of knowing the Savior of the world.[17] In the end, like Moses and many other believers throughout history,

---

[14] 2 Corinthians 11:21-33

[15] 2 Corinthians 1:7

[16] In 2 Timothy 1:12, the word know in the Greek is *oioda*. It is used to describe a confidence so sure that it is like believing that something has already taken place. This eternal faith and trust brought Paul peace amidst his suffering which is why he said, "I know whom I have believed and am persuaded that He is able to keep what I have committed to Him until that Day."

[17] Philippians 3:8-10

Paul chose to suffer affliction rather than enjoy the passing pleasures of sin.[18] He embraced the reality that God's promises and *God Himself* were higher pleasures.

Likewise, in his first epistle, Peter echoes Paul's theology[19] on suffering, and calls Christians to understand the purposes of suffering. The apostle Peter wrote his letters in obedience to two specific commands from Jesus which were to encourage and strengthen the brethren [believers], and to feed the flock [church] of God.[20] Peter was chastened by years of hardships, but found strength and considered his suffering a blessing for the sake of righteousness.[21] In other words, Peter believed God and knew that his present suffering would give him an opportunity to focus on eternity.[22] So at the end of his letter, he encouraged the church to be steadfast in their suffering knowing that it would perfect, establish, strengthen, and restore them.[23]

Similar to Paul and Peter, many individuals in

---

[18] Hebrews 11:25

[19] "Theos" means God and an "iology" means study of. Theology is therefore the study of God and seeks to ask questions such as, "how did everything get here?" Genesis 1:1 is a good place to start.

[20] Luke 22:32; John 21:15-17

[21] 1 Peter 3:14

[22] 1 Peter 4:16

[23] 1 Peter 5:10

Huruma village have experienced suffering, and their attitude and patience are a constant, humbling example to me.[24] God continues to use the sufferings of the saints for specific purposes. What then are the purposes that God still allows suffering to exist?

Why Does God Allow Suffering?

In chapter seven of my book *Culture V. Christ: Pursuing the Biblical Truth of Marriage and Children*,[25] I highlighted eight reasons to biblically and practically answer the question, "Why do bad things happen?" My intent was to help people understand that God allowing suffering in this world is not in vain. His ways are not our ways.[26] At the same time, a short study on the theology of suffering according to God's Word will help us know how to respond to suffering in an effective manner.

The longer you live, the more you realize that everyone is suffering in some shape or form. The

---

[24] See James 5:10

[25] Prichard, Charles. *Culture V. Christ: Pursuing the Biblical Truth of Marriage and Children*. Bloomington, IN: WestBow Press, 2014. Print. (See pages 104-112).

[26] Isaiah 55:8

hardships of life are at times inescapable. But, what are the reasons why God allows suffering?[27]

Reason #1—Ongoing *Sanctification*

The word sanctification is derived from two Latin words: *sanctus* (holy) and *ficare* (make). The idea is that according to Scripture, sanctification is how God *calls* us and *makes* us holy. To explain this, it is helpful to understand the English language and how indicatives and imperatives are used in Scripture.

An indicative (as it sounds) indicates what something is. For example, "That chair is brown." In the context of Scripture it is, "What God *has* done." An imperative is something you do. For example, "I am going to sit in the chair." In the Bible, the authors use imperatives to show what Christians are empowered to *do* because of what God *has already done* for them.

It is important as Christians that we don't place the imperatives in our life before the indicatives. In other words, we can't be sanctified (made holy) in Christ if we are not saved by Him in the first place. As a simple example, Peter quotes an Old Testament

---

[27] This list of four reasons for suffering is not all-encompassing. I attempted to take multiple passages of Scripture and group them into four broad categories that explain the reasons why God allows suffering.

passage and reminds the church to be holy in "all your conduct" *because* God is holy.[28] This "be holy" is an imperative. However, he knows that a person cannot be holy unless he is saved and redeemed through God's grace. So, Peter presents the believers an indicative and says that they [Christians] are a, "holy nation and a royal priesthood."[29] To put things into proper perspective, we cannot *be* sanctified unless we are *in Christ*. When you know who you are in Christ, you know what to do (see Matthew 4:1-11). In other words, the imperatives of the Christian life (i.e. stuff God says we are to do) manifest themselves *from* the indicatives.

A word of caution: because of our tendency toward works based righteousness, we still try to place the imperatives before the indicatives. In other words, works based righteousness and religion will say, "I'm going to do the imperatives so that I can achieve the indicatives" or "I am going to obey God, and therefore, He is going to accept me into His royal priesthood." However, Christianity is the other way around. We are accepted by God by grace through faith, in Jesus Christ and therefore, we obey God joyfully out of our love and gratitude to Him.[30]

The crucial key is to remember that we can be

---

[28] 1 Peter 1:15-16

[29] 1 Peter 2:9

[30] See Galatians 2:16-19; 1 John 5:1-5

sanctified through our suffering, if we allow God to do the work in our lives. Simply put, it's a choice. We can either choose to respond in faith and trust God knowing that sanctification is at work, or we can reject it. We must understand that suffering is really the training of our Father who loves us so much that He shares His holiness with us. Even though no discipline or training seems pleasant at the moment, it later produces fruit of righteousness, which God graciously gives to his children.[31]

While the word discipline or chastening is usually perceived in a negative context, the connotation in Scripture means nurturing and instructing. The writer of Hebrews says that, "Now no chastening seems to be joyful for the present, but painful; nevertheless, afterward it yields the peaceable fruit of righteousness to those who have been trained by it" (Hebrews 12:11). The Greek word for chastening is *paideia,* which is where we get the word pediatrics. Moreover, the Greek word for training is *gymnazō,* where the word gymnasium is derived. Like an athlete who exercises disciplined training habits, God's children can allow suffering to make them stronger.

---

[31] Hebrews 12:6, 10-11

Reason #2—*Sharing*

My wife and I lost a child before he was born and experienced tremendous pain. A young man (we'll call him David) who I discipled for three years lost his mother when she was murdered, and to make matters worse, David never knew his father. On the other side of the globe, Mutua from Kenya also experienced great pain by losing his mother when she died, leaving him orphaned and in severe poverty.

As a result of our respective pain in our journey of life, we each have the capacity to connect with others who have or are experiencing that same pain. For example, since we lost our child, we have been able to comfort and relate to other couples who have traveled the same hard road of life. As a single man, David volunteers at boys' homes and ministers to troubled teenagers who have been neglected by their parents. To be in parallel to this ability to relate and connect, I know Mutua is also able to minister to others in Huruma who've also lost family members and like him, have to shoulder the responsibility of caring for their family.

God is not only the "Father of mercies" but also the "God of all comfort." He knows us. He loves us. Do you run to Him for comfort? He is able to comfort us in all of our hardships. He does this so that we may comfort others who are suffering.[32]

Have you ever seen hardships this way? When suffering inevitably happens in your life, do you think, "Maybe God is allowing this to happen so that I will be a future comforter to someone who will (or has) experienced a similar trial?" As His children, God can give us discernment and wisdom to share with others amidst our suffering. In our suffering, we can experience God's love, goodness, and comfort. Do we share the characteristics of God with others? Do we share His love with others while they are suffering? Do we take the time to comfort others (even strangers) while they are suffering? Do you see that God allows us to suffer for other's sakes?

Reason #3—Genuine *Self-Refection*

The apostles record Jesus healing many people from physical and, even more importantly, spiritual sickness. Before restoring the man's sight, Jesus engaged with a man who was blind since birth. Jesus' disciples thought that the man was sightless because of either his own sin or his parents' sin. Jesus responded with, "Neither this man nor his parents sinned, but that the works of God should be revealed in him" (John 9:3). While the disciples and many

---

[32] 2 Corinthians 1:3-4

times the Pharisees were wrong in their thinking, it's interesting to see that they often attempted to answer the question of "Why suffering?" Similarly, when we are brought down by sickness or hardship, we too, have a tendency to think with an eternal mindset.

This genuine self-reflection should lead us closer to God as we realize how temporary life on earth actually is. God also uses suffering to call us to repentance and to turn from anything that we are treasuring on earth above God.[33] King David knew the importance of self-reflection. In Psalm 139, he asked God to search him and reveal to him any unrepentant sin in his life.[34] In Psalm 51, we see how repentant David later became.

What about you? Do you allow suffering to cause you to shake your fist and blame God or others? Or do you allow God to use your suffering to bring you to your knees and seek Him? Do you self-reflect or do you become self-centered?

Reason # 4—Tangible *Security*

Suffering automatically puts us in a position of insecurity. We either choose to respond in hopelessness, or we realize that God uses suffering to highlight our dependence and reliance on Him.

---

[33] See Luke 13:1-5

[34] Psalm 139:23-24

We don't *become* dependent on God, because we are *always* dependent on His hand in our lives. Apart from Him, we can't do anything because He is life.[35] God always uses suffering to call us to fully trust in Him instead of the fleeting and temporary things of the world.[36]

The reality is that we can't even compare suffering to the future glory we have as children of God. An eternal perspective (one that focuses on God) makes suffering endurable in this life. God is transforming us into His image as He moves us from one degree of glory to another.[37] In other words, if we observe, see, and focus on the glory of God rather than our suffering, we will experience tangible security in His hands as He transforms us.

This future reward of glory in Christ's presence is incomparable to the light, momentary affliction that you are experiencing at this moment. This suffering in a Christian's life is working for us a greater and "far more exceeding and eternal weight of glory" (2 Corinthians 4:17). Paul says that all horrifically painful suffering is considered light when we compare it to heaven. Eternity is a lot longer than our time on earth and so our suffering always lasts for only a moment in time.

---

[35] John 15:5

[36] See 2 Corinthians 1:8-9

[37] 2 Corinthians 3:18

You see, suffering works for us a great reward that will make up every loss here on earth an eternity-fold. In your suffering, consider the prize of seeing God in a different light—the prize of future eternal glory with Him. Do you see the future and tangible security that you will receive if you are His child? As a Christian, this fuels me to perceive suffering as temporary and incomparable to being in His presence forever![38]

Purposeful Understanding

It's undeniable that suffering is painful. The word suffer is many times a translation of the Greek word *lypeō*. This word means to distress, cause pain, sorrow or grief. Suffering is hard and perplexing, but is also purposeful. Its chief purpose is to conform us to the image of Christ.[39] So like Paul, we press on toward the goal.[40] Like soldiers in God's kingdom, we are at war.[41] We will suffer in this life,[42] but, "If we [are saved as his children] and died with Him, we shall

---

[38] See Psalm 16:11; John 17:3; 1 Corinthians 2:9; Philippians 1:21-23; Revelation 21:4

[39] Romans 8:28-31

[40] Philippians 3:12-14

[41] 2 Timothy 2:3-4

[42] See John 16:33; Philippians 1:29; 2 Timothy 3:12; 1 Peter 1:6-7; 1 Peter 4:12

also live with Him [in heaven]. If we endure [the hardships of this life], we shall also reign with Him" (2 Timothy 2:11-12).

My dear friends, don't waste your sufferings. Don't waste them! Don't allow the disasters of this world to cause you to despair. Find joy, peace, and even comfort and patiently see how God will use the hardships in your life for a greater purpose. Your sufferings are not working against you (unless you allow them to); they are working for you—producing an eternal weight of glory.[43]

Helen Berhane of Eritrea (a country in the southeastern horn of Africa) was severely tortured because of her faith in Jesus. Many of her family members had endured starvation, solitary confinement, beatings, electric shocks, and sexual abuse over the last decade. When interviewed by the Voice of the Martyrs Ministry team in Eritrea, she said, "On reflection, I think the authorities should understand by now that what they are doing doesn't work. I am convinced that the number of Christians [in Eritrea] has doubled or tripled since they closed the churches. So perhaps God is using this terrible situation for His glory."[44] Helen understands the purposes of suffering, and she knows how to respond.

---

[43] 2 Corinthians 4:17

[44] Waters, Michelle. *Eritrea: A People Imprisoned.* Bartlesville, OK: Living Sacrifice Book Company, 2012. Print. See also

So, how should we respond when hardships happen in our own lives? Moreover, how should we counsel others who are currently facing a wall that seems impossible to climb?

Responding to Suffering

Monte Williams, the assistant coach of the NBA Oklahoma City Thunder received word that his wife had just died in a car crash. The police said the driver was speeding 52 miles-per-hour over the limit. He crossed the centerline and hit her vehicle head-on. The 44-year-old mother of five, died shortly after arriving at the hospital. Three of their children were also in her car. They survived with multiple injuries.[45] The week after her death, Monte gave a powerful eulogy during his wife's funeral that shocked those who were in attendance.

How would you respond if you received that phone call, and then witnessed your wife die in front of your eyes at the hospital? Knowing God is in control of life and that hardships are not in vain, Monte responded at his wife's funeral by saying:

---

www.persecution.com for more information on the Voice of the Martyrs Ministry.

[45] See www.koco.com/news/vehicle-that-crashed-into-ingrid-williams-vehicle-was-going-92-mph-just-before-crash/38023774 for the police and news report of the accident.

"What we've gone through is pretty tough, and it's hard, and we want an answer, and we don't always get that answer when we want it, but we can't lose sight of the fact that God loves us, and that's what my wife [lived to], and that's what I try to, however badly, exhibit on a daily basis."

Monte knew Jesus. He knew that the love and mercy of God was able to bring him comfort in his grief as he mourned over his wife that day. He continued by saying:

"Let's not lose sight of what's important. God will work this out. My wife is in heaven. God is love. And when we walk away from this place today, let's celebrate, because my wife is where we all need to be, and I'm envious of that...We didn't lose [my wife]. When you lose something, you can't find it. I know exactly where my wife is [so] let's not lose sight of what's important. God is important. What Christ did on the cross is important."[46]

Rather than becoming bitter, having self-pity, displaying despair, or showing "justified" hatred toward the person who caused the car wreck, Mr. Williams continues to press on and see the tragedy through the lens of Scripture and His Savior. If you haven't yet, I encourage you to listen to the entire eulogy (see footnote for website), which shows the

---

[46] See www.nba.com/thunder/video/wordofthanks_williams_160 218 for a recording of the eulogy.

power of Christ as He comforts and forgives us so that we can do the same to others.

As shown by this testimony, a godly response to suffering is learned. In light of suffering, our human response is to doubt God's goodness, love, and care. When we read the historical records of Paul, we see that his response to suffering was learned over time. Sanctification is an ongoing process, not a one-time experience. Scripture is clear that we are saved *and* sanctified by our faith in Jesus.[47] At times we feel like we are in a valley (and we are). God wants us to look up and see Him because the reality is, we see mountains more plainly from a valley viewpoint. Remember, suffering is *never* meaningless. Suffering is always doing something in you, something you usually can't see or even begin to understand at the moment.[48]

From a biblical and historical perspective, we can look to the apostle Paul's life as an indication of how we should respond to suffering in our own lives. Luke, a doctor and historian, recorded Paul's journey from Troas to the colonial city of Philippi in Macedonia. After seeing a woman named Lydia come to know the Lord, Paul went outside into the city to pray. While traveling through the city, he and his

---

[47] Galatians 3:3-5
[48] 2 Corinthians 4:17

companion Silas were arrested, dragged through the marketplace, and placed before the magistrates. They were falsely accused of causing trouble in the city and breaking Jewish customs. After being beaten with rods and whipped 39 times, they were thrown into the lower part of the prison with their feet fastened to the ground.[49]

How did they respond? Luke said that, "At midnight, Paul and Silas were praying and singing hymns to God" (Acts 16:25). If you have not read this historic account of Paul and Silas while they were in jail, please do! These men of God responded to their unjust treatment by worshipping the King. They sang praises to the living God whom they knew and loved, the God that saved Paul and Silas from their sin. We see from this testimony that worship restored their joy.[50]

Again, I ask you, how do you respond to your circumstances? Read about Job's response when everything (including his children) was taken from him (Job 1:20-21). Job mourned, but more importantly, he responded in worship. We know that out of the mouth, the heart of a person speaks.[51] After his own wife tormented him and asked why he didn't curse God for his suffering, Job responded

---

[49] Acts 16:1-24

[50] Psalm 103:2

[51] Matthew 15:18

with, "shall we indeed accept good from God, and shall we not accept adversity" (Job 2:10)? Job found his hope in God and responded to his unthinkable hardships in a godly way.

Grow in Resilience

Consider this truth: your response to suffering is one of the few things that people cannot take away from you. While I was stationed at Robins Air Force Base, Georgia, I had the privilege of getting to know Air Force Brigadier General (retired) James Sehorn. General Sehorn was shot down over North Vietnam on December 14, 1967 and held as a Prisoner of War (POW) for five and a half years. Throughout the years of his incarceration, he withstood extreme mental and physical torture by ultimately trusting in God's promises. The last time I spoke with General Sehorn, I asked him how he was able to withstand such horrific suffering. He told me that he, along with other men in the POW camp, were able to survive through the strength they received from God.

These prisoners did not fear death because they knew Jesus. They possessed real hope. They sang worship songs while they were tortured, and their physical hardships were endured through the joy they had in Christ. Their enemies could not control their response.[52] Upon his release when the Vietnam War ended in 1973, General Sehorn prayed and praised God for "taking care of us for such a long time."[53]

So, is it wrong to cry out to God to relieve your suffering? Absolutely not! We are told to cast our anxiety and fear on God[54] and cry out to the Lord in our distress.[55] However, we have to understand and trust God's sovereignty and ways. Sometimes God pulls us out of a horrible situation or hardship, and sometimes He gives us the opportunity to endure and grow through the hardship.[56] Either way, our response is critical and reveals to the world the hope we have in Christ.

Consider the testimony of Annie Johnson Flint, born in 1886. Plagued with a number of diseases that eventually took her life, she wrote a hymn titled "He Giveth More Grace" shortly before her death in 1932. The words to a couple of the stanzas are:

---

[52] See www.youtube.com/watch?v=0KB7sGo30bE to watch an inspirational video of General James Sehorn speak to a group of chaplain candidates at Robins Air Force Base, GA.

[53] See www.pownetwork.org/bios/s/s016.htm to read some of General Sehorn's journal entries while he was a POW in Vietnam.

[54] 1 Peter 5:7

[55] Psalm 18:6

[56] Read the book of Daniel and compare his life to Stephen in Acts chapter 7

He giveth more grace as our burdens grow greater,
He sendeth more strength as our labors increase;
To added afflictions He addeth His mercy,
To multiplied trials He multiplies peace.
His love has no limits, His grace has no measure,
His power no boundary known unto men;
For out of His infinite riches in Jesus
He giveth, and giveth, and giveth again.[57]

Comfort and Peace

Having lived with some of the poorest people in the world, I have at times wondered if I am "serving God" when I find peace and comfort in my life. How can we discern whether or not our peace is from God, or a result of our disobedience? Let me explain.

We can, in fact, worship our own persecution, becoming self-righteous by experiencing levels of martyrdom. Paul's first letter to the Corinthian church explained the importance of motivation and love.[58] For Christians, persecution isn't always constant. Paul is an example of this truth. There were times throughout his Christian journey when he had plenty and when he was thrown in jail and stripped of everything he owned.[59] Regardless of the

---

[57] Lillenas Publishing Company, Kansas City, 1941.

[58] 1 Corinthians 13:3

[59] Philippians 4:11-13. Take note of the context of verse 13, which is frequently a misapplied or misunderstood "bumper sticker" verse in the church today.

circumstances, he was content in every situation God allowed while he preached the saving truth of Jesus Christ. We will discuss the topic of contentment and how it relates to poverty, suffering, and hope in a later chapter of this book.

While recently reading through the book of Mark, I noticed that Jesus told his disciples to rest because persecution was coming later.[60] Clearly, there are moments and even seasons when God wants us to experience comfort in order for us to rest, reflect, and prepare for future hardships. So, if we find our ultimate joy in God, we can enjoy the life He has given us as we know there will be a time to sing, laugh, dance, mourn…etc.[61] Is your life peaceful because God is granting you a time to rest, or does the peace result from your disobedience and keeping quiet, perhaps from being ashamed of your faith, the gospel, or Jesus?

While comfort and peace are not a sin, we have a tendency to turn comfort into a sin in our daily walk through life. I see it all too frequently in my own life—the desire for comfort can make me complacent with my "spiritual growth", and I choose comfort over obedience. It is not only possible but extremely likely for a materialistic society to worship comfort.

---

[60] Mark 6:31

[61] Ecclesiastes 3:12-13

This form of idolatry is especially offensive to God who has promised His children that He will take care of us on earth, or take us home to glory.[62]

Finally, remember that God uses suffering to strengthen and test our faith.[63] God wants us to rely on Him and not be deceived that we can "make it through the day" by our own resources. Though our outer bodies are dying, God is renewing and sanctifying our inner self.[64] At times, we forget or perhaps have never realized that He is our Rock, which cannot be moved. In our times of suffering, may we, like the psalmist cry out to God and say:

> "Whom have I in heaven but You?
> And there is none upon earth that I desire besides You.
> My flesh and my heart fail;
> But God is the strength of my heart and my portion
> forever" (Psalm 73:25-26).

---

[62] See Matthew 6:31-33, 7:11; Luke 12:24; Philippians 4:19

[63] James 1:2-3

[64] 2 Corinthians 4:16

Testimony – The Prayers of His Children

While at the church in Huruma Village, the congregation's pastor encouraged his flock with the verse Isaiah 40:31 which reads:

But those who wait on the Lord
Shall renew their strength;
They shall mount up with wings like eagles,
They shall run and not be weary,
They shall walk and not faint.

The following Sunday, I was given the honor of preaching the Word in the same church. After sharing what the Lord laid on my heart the night prior and singing praises to Jesus for over two hours, we began to pray. Listening to the prayers of God's people in Huruma brought me to tears. Simple yet poignant prayers such as, "Please help me to work hard today so that I may be able to feed my children this evening," and "Thank you, Father for giving us this land to sow and reap food."

Many of the children were constantly asking for food and milk, but were told to be patient and wait until evening when they were finally able to taste their first meal of the day. Despite their physical trials, the villagers experienced true peace in Christ while suffering extreme pain and hunger. Their physical needs did not detract them from worshipping their

King, who provided more than they could ask for or imagine (see Ephesians 3:20).

Personally, my inner person and physical realities often collide, not mesh. In contrast, that day I was witnessing God's children cry out to Him the way a child asks his father for help. Yet also in the same setting, I heard the same people cry out in desperation to surrender their lives to a God who has prepared a place for them in eternity where suffering, death, sickness, and even pain would be removed.

> "And God will wipe away every tear from their eyes; there shall be no more death, nor sorrow, nor crying. There shall be no more pain, for the former things have passed away" (Revelation 21:4).

Questions for Reflection

1. What is your tendency *when* suffering or hardships plague your life?

2. Do you respond to suffering like the apostle Paul, Helen Berhane, Monte Williams, or Annie Johnson Flint? Or do you typically become angry, self-pitied, bitter, and mean-spirited?

3. Why do you think you respond to suffering the way you do?

Verses to Memorize

2 Corinthians 4:7
Romans 5:3-5
Psalm 73:25-26

CHAPTER 2

Faith and Hope

Rejoice in hope, [be] patient in tribulation, continuing steadfastly in prayer.

—Romans 12:12

Never be afraid to trust an unknown future to a known God.

—Corrie Ten Boom

How We Fight Sin and Satan

In *The Art of War*, Chinese military strategist and philosopher General Sun Tzu once said, "If you know the enemy and know yourself, you need not fear the result of a hundred battles. If you know yourself but not the enemy, for every victory gained you will also suffer a defeat. If you know neither the enemy nor yourself, you will succumb in every battle."[65] In many military strategic studies classes in the United States, students remember this quote by the simplified version: "Know thy enemy, know thyself."

Knowing the Enemy

A dear friend of mine calls this "honoring the threat."[66] The threat is Satan. In his pride and sinful pursuit to become equal with God, he was cast down to earth where he now lives as an invisible and organized force of evil in the spiritual realms.[67] As we perceive from the fall, Satan is a great deceiver who is on the prowl to destroy us, as he disguises himself

---

[65] Giles, Lionel. *The Art of War: Sun Tzu*. Blacksburg, VA: Thrifty Books, 2009. Print.

[66] Thank you Paul Maykish for encouraging me to "honor the threat" while we studied the armor of God.

[67] Isaiah 14:12-13, Ephesians 6:12

as an angel of light.[68] He never forces us to sin but entices, lures, and pulls us to sin through *our own* evil desires.[69] He is after our hearts, and so we must resist him by putting on our spiritual armor.[70]

Scripture is clear that Satan uses suffering to tempt us to sin. Again, we can claim victory in this battle by putting on the full armor of God. Our armor includes: truth (our belt), righteousness (our breastplate), the gospel of peace (our shoes), salvation (our helmet), the Word of God (our sword), and *above all*, faith (our shield).[71] According to God's Word as spoken through Paul, our main armor is our faith as a weapon of defense, and the Word of God, along with prayer,[72] as our only offensive weapon.

Satan attacks our faith and without faith, we take the bait, fall into temptation, and sin, which ultimately, leads to death if left unchecked.[73] So in order to win the daily battle against our flesh and our enemies, we must stand firm and steadfast in our faith, our shield against the arrows (schemes) of Satan.[74] The best way to fight this enemy is to

---

[68] See Genesis 3:1-6; 1 Peter 5:8; John 10:10; 2 Corinthians 11:14

[69] James 1:14

[70] James 4:7, Ephesians 6:12-18

[71] Ephesians 6:10-20

[72] Ephesians 6:18

[73] Hebrews 11:6

[74] 2 Corinthians 2:10-11

strengthen what he is trying to destroy in us—our faith. We must resist him, refuse to give him any opportunities, and take a stand.[75] So I urge you as the psalmist writes to, "train your hands for war, and your fingers for battle" (Psalm 144:1).

Knowing Yourself

Along with knowing our enemy, we have to know about ourselves.

Satan understands that many people only trust or believe in God when things are going well. God has allowed this attack on faith just as He permitted Satan to target and test Job.[76] As humans, we tend to praise God in our health and curse God in our hardships. Again, this was Satan's aim when he sought to destroy God's servant.[77] While Satan is the great accuser[78] and tempts us to doubt God's goodness, we must understand that his main goal is to attack our faith and separate us from God. He knows his time is short and his power is limited[79] as the "god of this world" (2 Corinthians 4:4).

---

[75] James 4:7; 1 Peter 5:9, Ephesians 4:27, 6:11

[76] Job 1:10-11

[77] See Job 2:1-7

[78] Zechariah 3:1; Revelation 12:10

[79] See Revelation 12:12. We see throughout the book of Revelation (13:5, 7) and Job, that God is the one who "grants" Satan power.

As Christians, we all will suffer. In fact, if we don't, how can we call ourselves disciples? We should not be surprised when we suffer as though "some strange thing happened to [us]" (1 Peter 4:12). We expect it as we follow Jesus, who said in Matthew 10:22 that we would be hated and persecuted for His name's sake as we pursue holiness.[80] This makes sense because we know that the light of Christ does not mix with the darkness of sin and therefore, conflict ensues.[81]

Brothers and sisters, we are called to God's eternal glory (even amidst our suffering), which we only experience for a short while. He then perfects, establishes, and strengthens our faith in Him through His perfect goodness.[82] This is why we fight the good fight of faith.[83] We are prone to idolize comfort. We are prone to wander from our faith. As such, it is vital that we know the enemy and ourselves.

Satan is under God's control and serves His purposes in His sovereign plan of redemption (see Revelation 20:1-3).

[80] 2 Timothy 3:12
[81] John 3:20-21
[82] 1 Peter 5:9-10
[83] 1 Timothy 6:12

Rejoicing in Hope

God's promises give us real hope. God's abundance and richness of mercy[84] gives me as a Christian, hope that He who began a good work in me *will* bring it to completion when He returns because I am a partaker of His grace.[85] I have an eternal hope because I am born again.[86] I am not just changed; I am a whole new creation.[87]

God's mercy provides the Christian a hope through Christ and His resurrection.[88] The world thinks hope is found in those who have more material, physical, or mental abilities. The reality is that genuine, unwavering hope is found in the God of hope—Jesus Christ.[89] We can rejoice in this living hope of salvation that Jesus promised.[90] Like Paul and Silas while they were in prison, we can sing praises to God knowing His goodness never fails. As the psalmist said:

> Behold, the eye of the Lord is on those who fear Him,
> On those who hope in His mercy,
> To deliver their soul from death,

---

[84] Ephesians 2:4-7

[85] Philippians 1:6

[86] See John 3:1-21

[87] Galatians 2:20; 2 Corinthians 5:17

[88] 1 Peter 1:3-5

[89] Romans 15:13

[90] Romans 12:12; John 11:25

And to keep them alive in famine.

Our soul waits for the Lord;
He is our help and our shield.
For our heart shall rejoice in Him,
Because we have trusted in His holy name.

Let Your mercy, O Lord, be upon us,
Just as we hope in You (Psalm 33:18-22).

Helmet of Hope?

"Where is your helmet, Basic!"

I heard this phrase shouted by military cadre more than once while I was attending basic military training (BMT) at age 17, after graduating high school. Rather than politely ask a new trainee (basic) to calmly place his helmet on his head, this phrase was literally yelled in order to point out the importance of the helmet. A soldier's helmet is many times the very thing that saves him from a bullet or shrapnel from an explosive. This is why you witness service men and women grab their helmets while they run across the battlefield. A soldier's helmet protects his brain, because he knows that a shot to the head can cause death.

From a spiritual standpoint, the apostle Paul twice makes a connection between a military helmet and the hope of salvation. Faith in Christ gives us an eternal hope of salvation and eternal life.[91] As we focus our mind and thoughts on Him, our perspectives on suffering change.[92] Like a POW, we are still living as long as our hope, or helmet of salvation remains intact. As a brother in Christ of mine wrote,

> "This hope-helmet is made from the most firm and unchanging metals known to man. Your hope of salvation is rooted in the promise of God to save you (Hebrews 6:19); in the very blood of God which He shed for your sins (Matthew 26:28); in the Word of God which never changes (John 17:17); in the Spirit of God (2 Corinthians 5:5); in over 300 Old Testament prophecies of God which Jesus fulfilled (2 Peter 1:19); in the Will of God to have you Home (Luke 15:24); in the plan of God to redeem you (Hebrews 6:17); in His Divine character which loves you (John 3:16); in His faithfulness to never leave you (2 Timothy 2:11); and in the power of God to overcome and destroy the gates of hell (Matthew 16:18). Your hope of salvation is the most secure thing in this world. As you follow Him, this hope grows from strength to strength."[93]

So where is your helmet? If you too are a child of God, then the light, momentary troubles and afflictions that you are currently experiencing will never compare to the reality of spending eternity in paradise with our Lord.[94] As Christians, we are justified by His grace and have received the hope,

---

[91] See 1 Thessalonians 5:8; Ephesians 6:17

[92] Colossians 3:1-3

[93] Paul Maykish in his study on "The Helmet" from Ephesians 6:17

[94] 2 Corinthians 4:17; John 14:1-3

faith, and assurance of eternal life in Him.[95] This hope fuels our comfort as we wait with endurance for the glory of eternal life.

Endurance

> "For we know that the whole creation groans and labors with birth pangs together until now. Not only that, but we also who have the first fruits of the Spirit, even we ourselves groan within ourselves, eagerly waiting for the adoption, the redemption of our body. For we were saved in this hope, but hope that is seen is not hope; for why does one still hope for what he sees? But if we hope for what we do not see, we eagerly wait for it with perseverance" (Romans 8:22-25).

When I think about endurance, I imagine a long-distance runner who continues to push his body beyond its physical capabilities. Stride after stride, his body aches with pain, but he must refuse to quit the race for if he quits, he gains nothing. The spiritual race of life is similar. We must run, fight, and wait patiently with hope because we know that the race will eventually end. As the writer of Hebrews said, "let us throw off everything that hinders and the sin that so easily entangles. And let us run with perseverance the race marked out for us" (Hebrews 12:1b).

When dealing with suffering, it's easy to discuss it, but difficult to live out the biblical virtue of endurance.

---

[95] Titus 3:7; Hebrews 11:1

We are told in Scripture that those who endure hardships and temptation to sin are counted as blessed because God's intentions in suffering are never in vain.[96] Remember, He makes, "all things work together for good to those who love God, to those who are the called according to His purpose" (Romans 8:28). Along with being blessed, those who endure should be commended for their faithfulness.[97] I think again of people I know who are trapped in poverty-stricken slums in Africa. Their physical, spiritual, mental, and social trials have not been easy to overcome. Only through their faith do they hold on to real hope and peace that surpasses all understanding—a peace that guards their hearts and minds—a peace that divests all worry and anxiety from a person's life.[98] As Paul urged his spiritual son, Timothy:

> "Remember that Jesus Christ, of the seed of David, was raised from the dead according to my gospel, for which I suffer trouble as an evildoer, even to the point of chains; but the word of God is not chained. Therefore I endure all things for the sake of the elect, that they also may obtain the salvation which is in Christ Jesus with eternal glory.
>
> This is a faithful saying:
> For if we died with Him,
> We shall also live with Him.

---

[96] James 5:11
[97] 1 Peter 2:19
[98] Philippians 4:6-7

If we endure,
We shall also reign with Him.
If we deny Him,
He also will deny us.
If we are faithless,
He remains faithful;
He cannot deny Himself" (2 Timothy 2:8-13).

Read 2 Timothy 2:8-13 again! If we die to ourselves and come to Jesus, Who alone has the power to save, we will live. If we endure the hardships of this life, we will reign with Him in heaven. May we never reject the God who gives us the faith and hope so that we may endure and overcome our suffering.[99] Genuine hope in God is the only thing that will give those who are hopeless the ability to think that life is worth living.[100]

Patience

I struggle with patience immensely. Okay, let me just say it bluntly: I hate waiting! Just ask my wife

---

[99] See 2 Peter 1:1, Philippians 1:29, and Acts 3:16 where Scripture shows us that faith is from God.

[100] The American Association of Suicidology estimated in 2012 (and the numbers continue to rise) that there is a suicide attempt in the United States every 31 seconds. They also reported over 40,000 confirmed suicides this year alone. Suicide often occurs when a person falsely believes he has no hope. www.suicidology.org/resources/facts-statistics

who will tell you that I am "always on the go." The main reason why I dislike theme parks is because I don't like to stand in long lines (or any lines for that matter). I could come up with a list of excuses (oldest son, military, type-A personality…etc.), but it wouldn't justify the fact that I need to learn to be more patient.

When I am right in the middle of a hardship and don't know the outcome, I am almost always tempted to become fiercely impatient. I pray. No answer. I pray some more, and still God seems to remain silent. As a person who tends to see things as black and white, I long for either a "yes" or a "no" from God—not a "wait."

My ultimate problem in this struggle of patience is my immature faith. We cannot and should not have faith solely in God's promises, or even in our future circumstances, but in God Himself. Our faith strengthens when we hold on to our Creator, who will always provide everything we need. Maybe God is making me wait through a trial so that I will realize my dependence on Him.[101] Or perhaps He is allowing hardships in my life to forge my faith and relationship with the only One who can take away my deepest burdens.[102] Or even still, He may want me to realize that waiting develops patience, and is not ultimately

---

[101] See Proverbs 19:21
[102] Matthew 11:28

about what I get, but who I become through the process. Like Abraham who did not hesitate or waver at the promise of God, we too, need to allow God to strengthen our faith so that we can be completely convinced that God will do what He has promised.[103]

Think about a trial (big or small) in your life right now. What's your goal in the trial? Is your goal to "fix" your circumstance or situation? This may be dangerous territory. It is easy to lose sight of God's sovereignty and allow the hardship or trial to take over our life to a point where we fail to learn patience, and grow in becoming Christ-like. As James said, "My brethren, count it all joy when you fall into various trials, knowing that the testing of your faith produces patience. But let patience have its perfect work, that you may be perfect and complete, lacking nothing" (James 1:2-4).

Malcolm Muggeridge said it this way, "I look back on experiences that at the time seemed especially devastating and painful with particular satisfaction. Indeed, I can say with complete truthfulness that everything I have learned in my 75 years in this world, everything that has truly enhanced and enlightened my existence has been through affliction and not through happiness, whether pursued or attained."[104] When our life is

---

[103] Romans 4:20-21

[104] Malcolm Muggeridge, in *Homemade*, July, 1990

centered on God and not our circumstances, we can live a life of joy amidst the light and heavy trials.

Reflect on these verses from a beautiful song of endurance by Ginny Owens which she titled: "If You Want Me To"

> The pathway is broken
> And the signs are unclear
> And I don't know the reason
> Why You brought me here
>
> But just because You love me
> The way that You do
> I'm gonna walk through the valley
> If You want me to[105]

Will you walk through the valley if He wants you to? Are you putting on the full armor of God so that you can stand against your adversaries?[106] Will you be content in every circumstance whether you have plenty or nothing?[107]

---

[105] Owens, Ginny. *If You Want Me To: The Best of Ginny Owens.* Rocketown Records, 2006. CD.

[106] Ephesians 6:11-13

[107] Philippians 4:11-13

Testimony – Running with Faith

The fear of uncertainty can hold a powerful grip on those who live without physical abundance. Even with affluence, Satan tries to use the fear of the unknown to alter or even cripple our faith. Anasa Kirui refused to let the unknown stop him from fighting the good fight of faith.

During my quiet time with the Lord, I took a walk in a suburb near the capital city of Kenya when a young man (Anasa) approached me. He recently lost his garden (which provided all of his income) to a flood earlier that year. After sharing passages from Scripture about faith and trust in the Lord, he smiled. His countenance beamed with joy and peace and he walked in the opposite direction. As we parted ways, the last words I heard from him were, "My brother! Faith is not blind. My trust in Jesus has always given me sight to see His goodness in my life."

Hebrews chapter 11 records people throughout history who did not let uncertainty negatively affect their daily decisions. Like these heroes of faith, Anasa didn't allow uncertainty of what he could physically see in his life, to interfere with his confidence in what he could not see.

God's character doesn't change—and neither should our trust and faith in Him. We can stand on His promises with confidence, knowing that He is always at work for His glory and our joy in Him.

Questions for Reflection

1. Recall a time when you were in a valley. Did you despair or look to God for direction, comfort, and wisdom?

2. Define spiritual endurance in your own words.

3. Write down three characteristics of the enemy. How do you put your armor on and fight temptation daily?

4. How is hope connected to faith and endurance?

Verses to Memorize

Ephesians 6:14-18
1 Corinthians 10:13
1 Peter 1:3-5

CHAPTER 3

Seeking Contentment

I have learned in whatever state I am, to be content: I know how to be abased, and I know how to abound. Everywhere and in all things I have learned both to be full and to be hungry, both to abound and to suffer need. I can do all things through Christ who strengthens me.

—Philippians 4:11-13

Contentment makes poor men rich; discontent makes rich men poor.

—Benjamin Franklin

Contentment Defined

The term "contentment" is derived from the Greek word *arkeo*, which means to be enough, to be satisfied, and to be sufficient. In the context of Scripture, the idea of being sufficient refers to a person's met needs but not necessarily his wants. Jesus said that His grace is *always* sufficient for us because His strength is made perfect in our weakness.[108]

The truth of contentment begins with understanding that God will, "supply all your need according to His riches in glory by Christ Jesus" (Philippians 4:19). Moreover, we can rejoice when we have nothing physically, but possess everything in Christ.[109] Of course, needs, wants, and desires are regularly misunderstood and confused. In fact, the idea that God will give us whatever we want if we believe or have faith in Him (i.e. the "prosperity gospel"), is a dangerous and abominable doctrine that has plagued and misguided so many Christians over the years.[110]

---

[108] 2 Corinthians 12:9

[109] See 1 Corinthians 3:21-23; 2 Corinthians 6:4-10

[110] See www.desiringgod.org/interviews/why-i-abominate-the-prosperity-gospel

Contentment through Christ

"But I rejoiced in the Lord greatly that now at last your care for me has flourished again; though you surely did care, but you lacked opportunity. Not that I speak in regard to need, for I have learned in whatever state I am, to be content: I know how to be abased, and I know how to abound. Everywhere and in all things I have learned both to be full and to be hungry, both to abound and to suffer need. I can do all things through Christ who strengthens me. Nevertheless you have done well that you shared in my distress" (Philippians 4:10-14).

I love this passage of Scripture! Paul encouraged the church in Philippi by speaking with authority that he had learned to be content. Contentment is not a natural characteristic. We see in the book of Philippians that God's sovereignty gives us reasons to trust Him and this brings contentment in our lives. We know that He will help us persevere in our trials as He uses them to further spread the gospel and His glory.[111] Moreover, faith and suffering are part of God's perfect will, since we have been granted to believe in Him and suffer for His sake.[112] In all of this, God is providing all of our needs—this should lead us to contentment in Him as we trust in His promises with thankful hearts.[113] Do you see that?

---

[111] Philippians 1:6, 12

[112] Philippians 1:29

[113] Philippians 4:19

Contentment through Christ allows us to be thankful and rejoice—always!

Prosperity without Enjoyment

Vanity. Meaninglessness. Emptiness. Apart from enjoyment, all prosperity is worthless. God provides all things to mankind—along with the joy to take delight in them. A young man from Uganda once told me that an individual may possess everything and yet enjoy nothing. He was referring to a passage in Ecclesiastes where King Solomon gives us the secret to prosperity. It reads, "a man to whom God has given riches and wealth and honor, so that he lacks nothing for himself of all he desires; yet God does not give him power to eat of [enjoy] it…" (Ecclesiastes 6:2). In other words, our contentment in what God gives us, carries far more weight and allows us to fight through the temptation of despair, self-pity, and ungratefulness.

Again, contentment in God is the key to unlocking joy. We gain much when we live content lives, because we brought nothing into this world, and it is certain that we will take nothing physically with us into eternity.[114] Think about it. What does everyone ask for on their deathbed: their money, possessions, and

---

[114] 1 Timothy 6:6-7

trophies? No, they ask to be around those whom they love and care for. God tells us to be content with food in our stomach and clothing on our backs for this is what we need to survive.[115] Everything else is considered a luxury and should not be taken for granted. Oh, how easy it is to fall into the temptation of covetousness, which leads us to all kinds of evil and certain destruction.[116]

Joy is a Gift from God

God is the one who gives us enjoyment in life. Joy is purely a gift from God and not a result of any earthly riches. As King Solomon said, we can find joy in our daily work (labor) and simplistic living for, "every man to whom God has given riches and wealth and power, and given him power to eat of it, to receive his heritage and rejoice in his labor—this is the gift from God" (Ecclesiastes 5:19-20). This joy keeps us profitable from a holistic standpoint whether we have plenty or nothing.[117]

As followers of Christ, we should be goaded[118] into reflecting on the reality of the vaporous life we live

---

[115] 1 Timothy 6:8

[116] 1 Timothy 6:9-10

[117] Ecclesiastes 5:20; Philippians 4:12

[118] Solomon uses the term "goad" (which is a tool that farmers and shepherds use to prod animals) to reveal the reflections of

on earth, which appears and quickly vanishes.[119] Our understanding of possessions and dependency on God helps us focus our lives beyond the temporary, and instead, on the eternal and glorious joy of the universe—Jesus Christ. Any prosperity without the enjoyment, which God provides, is vanity. So contentment is far better than any form of prosperity. In other words, enjoying prosperity itself can lead to idolatry. God gives us good gifts but they are not to be worshipped.

The Effects of Discontentment

Solomon had everything the world values (cash, cars, and a huge harem). In today's day, it is estimated that his net worth would be over 100 billion dollars.[120] He had incredible potential as a wise king, an ingenious builder, and a genius administrator of the land under Israeli control at the time of his reign, from approximately 970-930 B.C.[121] Many biblical scholars believe that toward the end of his life, Solomon wrote the book of Ecclesiastes which asks

---

mankind and point us into eternal thinking and living. See Ecclesiastes 12:11.

[119] James 4:14

[120] See 1 Kings 10:14-29; 1 Kings 20-28

[121] See 1 Kings 3:16-27, 4:29-34, 10:1-7; 2 Kings 7-9; 1 Kings 4

the question, "What's the point of life" and answers it with, "Life is meaningless without God."

During this time in his life, you would have thought that Solomon was content since he possessed everything we humans may often want. Along with great wealth and power, Solomon was no fool. Even though he partied like a celebrity, built forests and a mighty kingdom, and purchased goods beyond measure,[122] King Solomon's "wisdom remained with [him]" (Ecclesiastes 2:9). In fact, history records him as the wisest man to ever live.[123] After years of not withholding any of his eyes' desires, Solomon, "looked on all the work that [his] hands had done… and indeed all was vanity and grasping for the wind. There was no [eternal or meaningful] profit" (Ecclesiastes 2:11). In other words, though this man had "gained the world"[124] his inner being was wasting away and so, he despaired.

Many people's lives are categorized by a sense of discontent. The answer is not to seek after more pleasure, possessions, positions, or prosperity. As we read and study the book of Ecclesiastes, clearly temporary treasures are worthless in the end. In fact, even their enjoyment is in vain apart from God. When we reflect upon the meaning of life without

---

[122] Ecclesiastes 2:1-8

[123] 1 Kings 3:11-14

[124] Matthew 16:26

God in the center, we despair. However, when we "fear God and keep His commands" (Ecclesiastes 12:13) we can meditate upon the beauty of life, and in our dependency, draw nearer to the One who gives, sustains, and truly blesses the life we live.

Blessed – According to Scripture

A glance at the Internet or social media outlets and you'll quickly find someone using the term "I'm blessed" or "Be blessed" as a sort of an undercover boastful phrase. How many times have you seen or read something where the term "blessed" is used synonymously with a "good" or "successful" life according to the world's standards? Many Christians say things like, *I'm blessed to have a good family; I'm blessed because I got a raise today; I'm blessed to have financial security or obedient children*…etc. We have a mindset that equates abundance, security, or comfort with blessings—but think about it. Even if (or when) someone has all these things: health, wealth, security, and comfort, are they truly blessed? Would this person feel dependent on God, or would he feel self-sufficient, proud, and unsatisfied with his life?

A person who experiences suffering, hardship, trials, and loss is more likely to seek God for His guidance and perfect will.[125] Solomon had *everything* that a person would want, and yet found it all to be temporary, unsatisfying, and meaningless in the end. Using a completely different Biblical character, Job is a perfect example of someone who was brought to his knees and was able to finally realize his utter dependence on God when everything was taken from him (health, wealth, family…etc.).[126]

To biblically define what it means to be blessed, we have to look at the translation of its original Greek word *Makarioi* which means to be fully satisfied. In Scripture, the word refers to those who receive God's favor. Interestingly enough, the New Testament uses the word "bless" "blessed" and "blessing" over 100 times and not once is it in reference to a material possession or prosperity. In Jesus' "Sermon on the Mount" in Matthew chapter five, we see that blessings come when we hear God's Word and obey it, and remain steadfast under trials and sufferings.[127] These are just as a few examples. In Scripture, blessings are almost always connected to our relationship with Jesus, or with poverty, sufferings, or trials.

We can easily conclude that to be truly and fully "blessed" is to be satisfied in Jesus Christ. Anything that draws us to Him; anything that allows (or forces)

---

[125] Romans 12:2

[126] See Job 1:13-22

[127] Luke 11:28; James 1:12

us to think about the reality of eternity; anything that causes us to look to Him as our supreme treasure—this is being blessed! This is why trials, suffering, hardships, and disappointments are usually the catalyst for receiving blessings or "being blessed." God's greatest blessing to mankind is Himself—He Who opened the door for us to find true satisfaction in His presence.[128]

A Great Inheritance

What if I told you that at the end of today, you would receive one billion dollars outright for no reason? Would your mood change? Of course! You would be excited, thankful, happy, and maybe even confused as to why this is happening to you. What if I told you that if you were a child of God, you will, in a short time, reign with Him and inherit the world? Compared to everything (the world), one billion dollars is nothing. Well, the reality is, if Jesus is your Lord and Savior, you will, in fact, receive this inheritance when He takes you home soon. I purposefully chose the word *soon* because even if you lived to be 100 years old, eternity is a lot longer.

As children of God, we will receive this great inheritance in a short time as heirs of the entire world.

---

[128] Psalm 16:11

Paul said that Jesus Christ owns all things.[129] When we are in Christ (who is the heir of everything), we also inherit the world. "Therefore let no one boast in men. For all things are yours: whether…the world or life or death, or things present or things to come—all are yours. And you are Christ's, and Christ is God's" (1 Corinthians 3:21-23). Christians will receive this great promise[130] if we have been grafted into the Vine.[131] So, what does it mean to be heirs of the world?

All things belong to God. He is the creator and sustainer of life and has "in these last days spoken to us by His Son [Jesus], whom He has appointed heir of all things, through whom also He made the worlds" (Hebrew 2:1-2). In other words, all things belong to Jesus, and if we are in Him as God's children, all things will belong to us as a great inheritance.

Dear brothers and sisters in Christ, you can be content in Him alone. Dear friends who do not know Christ, you *cannot* be content without Him. As Jesus said:

> "Do not lay up for yourselves treasures on earth, where moth and rust destroy and where thieves break in and steal; but lay up for yourselves treasures in heaven, where neither moth nor rust destroys and where thieves do not break in and steal. For where your treasure is, there your heart will be also" (Matthew 6:19-21).

---

[129] 1 Corinthians 15:25-27
[130] Galatians 3:29
[131] Romans 11:16-18

Testimony – Peace through Contentment

From Huruma Village, I journeyed seven kilometers (4.3 miles) to Kibera, the largest urban slum in Africa which houses over two and a half million who live in poverty. Standing on the tangential highway, my gaze overlooked the slum and its vastness stirred within me a sense of overwhelming fear. As I walked through the streets while humming a gospel hymn, a man surprisingly invited me into his home.

The very first thing I noticed in this Kenyan brother's home was a single broken window. It was clear to me that water poured into that part of his home when it rained. I asked how long his window had been broken and he told me it had been over two months. He was saving a little money every month to hopefully buy the necessary supplies for the repair one day.

This Kenyan Christian told me that he never found a reason to worry about his situation. Moreover, he evidentially found true contentment because God continued to provide his need of food and clothing. "Brother Charles, God commands us to be content with food and clothing," he told me. "A house is optional."

"But godliness with contentment is great gain, for we brought nothing into the world, and we cannot take anything out of the world. But if we have food and clothing, with these we will be content" (1 Timothy 6:6-7).

I was familiar with Jesus' parable in Matthew 6:25-34. We are commanded not to worry about what we will eat or wear. Our Father will sustain us in this life or call us to our eternal home. He promises food and clothing but shelter is a luxury. So we have to ask ourselves, are we content? Do we understand that contentment will bring us peace?

Questions for Reflection

1. Define contentment in your own words. Are you content in your life right now? If not, what areas are you discontent in? Why?

2. Do you think you can buy happiness? Or are happiness and joy a gift from God? What Bible verses can you reference to back up your thinking?

3. Who or what is the supreme joy in your life?

4. Are you truly blessed? How do you know?

Verses to Memorize

Hebrews 13:5
1 Timothy 6:6-8
2 Corinthians 6:10

CHAPTER 4

❖ ❖ ❖

A Right Mindset

If then you were raised with Christ, seek those things which are above, where Christ is, sitting at the right hand of God. Set your mind on things above, not on things on the earth.

—Colossians 3:1-2

If you read history you will find that the Christians who did most for the present world were precisely those who thought most of the next…It is since Christians have largely ceased to think of the other world that they have become so ineffective in this. Aim at heaven and you will get earth "thrown in": aim at earth and you will get neither.

—C.S. Lewis

Worldly Mindset

As a Christian, I am commanded by God and empowered by His Holy Spirit abiding in me to live my life with my mind set on eternity. Before I trusted in Jesus to save me from my trespasses and sin, I walked according to the ways of this world in utter rebellion and disobedience.[132] My only aim in life was to fulfill the desires of my wicked flesh and mind, as I was not a child of God, but a child of wrath in my conduct.[133] So much so, that if I could insert myself into Paul's letter to the Ephesians, it might read something like this:

> "But God, who is rich in mercy, because of His great love with which He loved [me], even when [I was] dead in trespasses, made [me] alive together with Christ (by grace [I] have been saved), and raised [me] up together, and made [me] sit together in the heavenly places in Christ Jesus, that in the ages to come He might show the exceeding riches of His grace in His kindness toward [me] in Christ Jesus. For by grace [I] have been saved through faith, and that not of [myself]; it is the gift of God, not of works, lest [I] should boast. For [now I am] His workmanship, created in Christ Jesus for good works, which God prepared beforehand that [I] should walk in them" (Ephesians 2:4-10).

As a result of this miracle in my life, I am emboldened to live a life that is honoring and pleasing

---

[132] Ephesians 2:1-2
[133] Ephesians 2:3

to my Father who is in heaven. By God's grace, I can only love God if I set my mind on things of the Spirit rather than things of my flesh.[134] The warnings from Scripture are clear that those who are carnal-minded are enemies of God and cannot please Him.[135] This leads to certain spiritual death and separation from the Life. As Jesus said, "I am the way, the truth, and the life. No one comes to the Father except through Me" (John 14:6). Know this, "If you live according to the flesh you will die; but if by the Spirit you put to death the deeds of the body, you will live" (Romans 8:13). Clearly, setting our mind on the Spirit sets the stage for how we live our life.

Heavenly Mindset

What does Paul mean in Romans chapter eight to set your mind on the Spirit? A mind that accords itself with the flesh produces a mind that is set on the flesh. The opposite is true with a life that lives according to the Spirit of God. This set mind is one that: inclines to, dwells on, prefers, or enjoys. In other words, a mind that is set on things of this world (or of mankind) will produce works or deeds that are worldly. The phrase, "things of the flesh" refers to

---

[134] Romans 8:5

[135] Romans 8:6-8

anything that is done without God. In the previous chapter, we discussed King Solomon in the book of Ecclesiastes. King Solomon repeatedly emphasizes that anything done without dependence and reliance on God is in vain because it is done in the flesh.[136] In contrast, we are told to set our mind on the things of God.

What does Paul mean by setting our minds on the things of the Spirit or on God? The things of the Spirit are things that bring God glory. Since what we think and speak about reveals what is in our heart,[137] we must understand the importance of controlling our thoughts. So we think of and meditate on things that are true, noble, just, pure, lovely, of good report, virtuous, and praiseworthy.[138] This is a good litmus test when you are wondering whether or not your thoughts are of God or of your flesh. It's like the old Christian phrase that needs to come back, *what would Jesus do?* Or maybe we should say, *what would Jesus think?* We all know that our thinking precedes our doing. Therefore, in order to live a life focused

---

[136] A helpful cross-reference is in Matthew 16:23 when Jesus rebukes Peter for trying to get in the way of His mission to die on the cross. He uses the same phrase that Paul uses in Romans 8 when He tells Peter that he was being mindful of the things of men rather than of God.

[137] Matthew 15:18

[138] Philippians 4:8

on the eternal rather than the temporary, we must possess a godly, eternal mindset.

Eternal Mindset

In 1956, when Jim Elliot and four other missionaries were killed by the Auca Indians in Ecuador while they were sharing the gospel, many saw the event as an awful tragedy. While it was hard to comprehend the sadness that came over the families of the murdered missionaries, many did not know that one of Jim's credos was, "He is no fool who gives up what he cannot keep to gain what he cannot lose."[139]

Jim Elliot lived his life with an eternal mindset. He did not worry about his earthly safety or security because he knew that as a child of God, he would wake up in the arms of the King upon his death. As Jesus said, "But seek first the kingdom of God and His righteousness, and all these things shall be added to you. Therefore do not worry about tomorrow, for tomorrow will worry about its own things. Sufficient for the day is its own trouble" (Matthew 6:33-34).

In contrast, we can read the historical account of

---

[139] Jim Elliot's testimony is incredible. The families that reached out to and loved the Auca tribe in Ecuador have powerful stories to share. I encourage you to look them up and watch the featured film "End of the Spear" directed by Jim Hanon.

a rich young ruler who walked away from Jesus with sadness in his countenance because he was unwilling to give up the temporary life he lived. When the young man asked Jesus what he needed to do to inherit eternal life, Jesus responded by asking him if had kept the law. The rich man responded in a self-righteous way and so Jesus said, "Go, sell what you have and give to the poor, and you will have treasure in heaven; and come, follow Me" (Matthew 19:21).

Jesus was after his heart. He was testing him to see if this young man was willing to let go of his earthly possessions (which the man idolized) in order to gain eternal life in Christ.[140] Had he responded to Jesus' call to be a follower, the inheritance that he would have gained would have never perished, faded, or spoiled; for eternity with God is far greater than eternity without Him.[141] Sadly, the rich young ruler tried to hold on to what he could not eternally possess and rejected what he could not eternally lose. He decided not to trade his fleeting possessions for salvation.

How does this eternal mindset help us with suffering? Jesus was obviously no stranger to suffering. As such we look to Him as the, "author and finisher of our faith, who for the joy that was set before Him

---

[140] 1 Corinthians 3:23; Ephesians 1:11; Colossians 3:24

[141] 1 Peter 1:4

endured the cross, despising the shame, and sat down at the right hand of the throne of God [when he conquered the grave]" (Hebrews 12:2). While it's our human nature to want to avoid hardship, we are reminded that trials are not such a burden because we can lay them at the feet of the cross and rejoice in them.[142] Our mindset on things of the Spirit rather than our circumstances, will help us experience joy in the midst of persecution. When our perspectives change, everyone around us will realize that our hope is in the Lord and not this temporary world.[143]

As the apostle Paul rightly said in a letter written to the church in Corinth:

> "And our hope for you is steadfast, because we know that as you are partakers of the sufferings, so also you will partake of the consolation" (2 Corinthians 1:7).

Paul continued his exhortation by saying:

> "Therefore we do not lose heart. Even though our outward man is perishing, yet the inward man is being renewed day by day. For our light affliction, which is but for a moment, is working for us a far more exceeding and eternal weight of glory, while we do not look at the things which are seen, but at the things which are not seen. For the things which are seen are temporary, but the things which are not seen are eternal" (2 Corinthians 4:16-18).

---

[142] James 1:2-3; Psalm 55:22

[143] See Psalm 37:9; 1 Timothy 4:10

Renew Your Mind

Renew your mind. Do not conform to the patterns of the world, but rather become transformed when your mind is renewed in Jesus Christ.[144] A Christian is an alien in this world and yet at the same time, we live in this world.[145] The saying is *we are in the world, but not of the world*. As Jesus said, "I do not pray that You should take them out of the world, but that You should keep them from the evil one. They are not of the world, just as I am not of the world" (John 17:15-16).

The Greek word for renew is *metemorphōthë* and it is used only one other time in the gospels. The word "renew" as seen in Scripture is the same word as "transfiguration". A prime example of this is in the gospel of Matthew, when "He [Jesus] was transfigured before them. His face shone like the sun, and His clothes became as white as the light" (Matthew 17:2).[146] We don't transform our minds by simply *avoiding* worldly (sinful) behavior; and we don't merely switch our "list of behaviors" to a "spiritual list" of good deeds. According to Scripture, our works of the flesh are replaced by the fruit of

---

[144] Romans 12:1

[145] See Philippians 3:20; 1 Peter 2:11

[146] See also Mark 9:2

the Spirit.[147] This is the difference between doing something right because you feel convicted and are worried about making a fool of yourself, and doing good out of the transformed person you are in Christ. Our heart should be to love others out of gratitude for Christ and His love for us. In summary, the transformation (renewal) of our mind is a change from the inside out.

Why do our minds need to be renewed? By nature, we have a debased mind as a result of our sin.[148] Because of this, our minds reject truth and worship ourselves instead of our Creator. To combat this, we must prepare our minds to walk in the truth. Consider Peter's take on our mindset when he says, "Therefore gird up the loins of your mind, be sober, and rest your hope fully upon the grace that is to be brought to you at the revelation of Jesus Christ; as obedient children, not conforming yourselves to the former lusts, as in your ignorance" (1 Peter 1:13-14).[149]

We know that our thinking controls our actions and emotions.[150] It becomes vital that we focus on renewing our mind daily.[151] When we flee from our "youthful passions," walk in the Spirit, and pursue

---

[147] See Galatians 5

[148] Romans 1:28

[149] See also Ephesians 4:17-18

[150] Proverbs 23:7

[151] Ephesians 4:23

the things of God (righteousness, peace, love, etc.),[152] by His grace, we can overcome our sinful desires, and our minds are renewed and transformed. This in turn, allows us to discern God's good, pleasing, and perfect will.[153]

Find God's Will

The term "God's will" is many times thrown around in Christian circles with little understanding or content. I've been asked the question probably close to 100 times, "What is God's will for my life?" To answer this question, it is helpful to walk through what I believe the Bible reveals are three broad categories of God's will.

The first "will of God" is the *sovereign will of God*. God is God. His ultimate plans will always come to pass as no one can hinder, compel, or stop Him. While mankind is given free will (freedom to choose right and wrong), we are not totally free to do whatever we please. Consider gravity as an example. No amount of freedom of the will allows a person to ignore natural law that God has established. God's

---

[152] 2 Timothy 2:22
[153] Romans 12:1-2

sovereign will is good, perfect, and pleasing[154] and so we never have to wonder if God is "up to no good."

The second is the *revealed will of God*. God has given us His Word and revealed to us His will through the Bible. He commands us not to lie, steal, cheat, or commit adultery. He commands us to love our neighbor, to include our enemies, and look out for others before ourselves. Obviously, these things do not always come to pass because mankind chooses to reject them and sin.

The third will is *using wisdom to act*. As we renew our minds and line up our desires with God's, we are able to seek His will when we make decisions. Of course, we make hundreds of decisions every day and most of our decisions are based on habit or character. When we are stuck and have to make a decision as to what job to take, spouse to marry, school to attend, etc., we can genuinely seek God for answers. We can test our pending decisions with the Word of God, and we can continue to walk in the Spirit of truth.

To summarize these three broad answers to God's Will, we see that our Father's will is that we will ultimately be *saved, spirit filled*, and *sanctified*.[155] That is God's desire. That is our aim; this must be our mindset as we understand, discern, and seek God's will.

---

[154] Romans 12:2

[155] 2 Peter 3:9; John 3:17; Ephesians 5:18-21; Colossians 3:16; 1 Thessalonians 4:7

Jesus' Mindset

When we really consider the idea of renewing our minds, we look to Jesus. Consider the implications of this passage in the book of Philippians:

> "Let this mind be in you which was also in Christ Jesus, who, being in the form of God, did not consider it robbery to be equal with God, but made Himself of no reputation, taking the form of a bondservant, and coming in the likeness of men. And being found in appearance as a man, He humbled Himself and became obedient to the point of death, even the death of the cross" (Philippians 2:5-8).

What was Jesus' mindset? What did He think about? As God who came to earth in the fullness of Man—without sin[156]—how did He look at situations in life?

Jesus said that He came down from heaven to do God's will.[157] Moreover, He said that he fed (figuratively speaking) on the food of doing the will of the Father.[158] He humbled Himself as He went about His Father's business.[159] This was Jesus' mindset as He fulfilled His ministry and conquered sin and death. Our work is to love God by obeying Him,

---

[156] 2 Corinthians 5:21; Hebrews 4:15; 1 Peter 2:22
[157] John 6:38
[158] John 4:34
[159] Luke 2:49

and loving others by putting their needs before our own.[160]

Contemplate John's account when Jesus raised his friend Lazarus from the dead. The Bible makes it clear that Jesus loved Lazarus and yet, He let Lazarus die so that God's glory could be revealed in a new way.[161] Why? How can love equate to letting someone die? God's purposes for allowing suffering (in this case sorrow from death) are beyond our understanding in the moment. In the case of Lazarus, his death was allowed so that others around him would believe in the saving power and Lordship of Jesus Christ, who miraculously raised him from the dead.[162] Jesus' mindset, even in the face of death, is one that we can marvel at as we too, seek to do good works that God has prepared in advance for us to accomplish.[163]

Understanding True Love

Christianity defines love in a radical way. God demonstrates His love ultimately by giving us what we need the most—Himself. Our supreme need from God is to experience God which we are able to experience because of what Christ did out of love for

---

[160] 1 John 5:1-5; Philippians 2:1-4

[161] John 11:4-5

[162] John 11:15

[163] Ephesians 2:10

us. The God of the universe "demonstrate[d] His own love toward us, in that while we were still sinners, Christ died for us" (Romans 5:8).

Think about it, the greatest possible being (God) expressed the greatest possible moral ethic (love) in the greatest possible way (self-sacrifice). He demonstrated all of this at the cross. He died for sinners. He died for you and me. We were children of wrath, rebellious against Him. While we sacrifice for those who love us back, God gave the ultimate sacrifice for those who hated Him. "For when we were still without strength, in due time Christ died for the ungodly. For scarcely for a righteous man will one die; yet perhaps for a good man someone would even dare to die" (Romans 5:6-7). Understanding God's love gives us hope in the midst of physical pain, suffering, and even death.

When we understand God's unfathomable love, we are free to love others more. We are free and empowered to love our enemies and bless those who curse us.[164] As the apostle John said in his letter to the church:

> "Beloved, let us love one another, for love is of God; and everyone who loves is born of God and knows God. He who does not love does not know God, for God is love. In this the love of God was manifested toward us, that God has sent His only begotten Son into the world, that we might live through Him. In this is love, not that we loved God, but that He loved us and sent His Son to be the propitiation for our

---

[164] Matthew 5:44

sins. Beloved, if God so loved us, we also ought to love one another" (1 John 4:7-11).

We need to see God's glory as our ultimate treasure, which as Christians, helps us respond with an eternal mindset to physical death and pain. This is what Paul means when he writes, "For me, to live is Christ, and to die is gain" (Philippians 1:21). Only children of God can say this and know that when they die, they will be in the presence of Christ. Only a Christian can experience true contentment on this earth, and at the same time, have a joyful longing for death—whenever Christ returns to take us home—for we will always be aliens of this world.

Take heart in the truth found in God's Word. And I hope you find encouragement in what Jane F. Crewdson penned in her hymn *There Is No Sorrow, Lord, Too Light*:

"There is no sorrow, Lord, too light
To bring in prayer to Thee;
There is no anxious care too slight
To wake Thy sympathy.

Thou, who hast trod the thorny road,
Wilt share each small distress;
The love, which bore the greater load,
Will not refuse the less.

There is no secret sigh we breathe,
But meets Thine ear divine;
And every cross grows light beneath
The shadow, Lord, of Thine.

Life's ills without, sin's strife within,
The heart would overflow,
But for that love which died for sin,
That love which wept with woe."

Testimony – Living for the King

Fourteen-year-old Ugandan Akina Himaya was walking back to her village home when a group of men ambushed her. She was beaten to the point of unconsciousness and then sexually molested. God met Akina in her pain as she cried out to Him for comfort.

I met Akina on her twenty-first birthday at a youth pastor's conference in Atlanta, Georgia. After sharing her story in more detail, I asked her how she was able to overcome the bitterness and hatred she had in her heart against the perpetrators that changed her life forever at such a young age. She quickly pointed me to a passage in John chapter eight.

The Pharisees and religious leaders had caught a woman who had committed adultery against her husband. In those days, corporate law required that the accused would be stoned to death. When the Pharisees asked Jesus for His verdict, the Son of God responded to them by saying, "He who is without sin among you, let him throw a stone at her first" (John 8:7b).

By God's grace, Akina was able to forgive those who wronged her because she understood her brokenness before a Holy God and didn't let anger, hatred, pride, or self-righteousness paralyze her. She understood that true love was demonstrated at the cross. In the midst of hardship, God reminded Akina that a forgiving heart freed her to live for the King.

Questions for Reflection

1. Is your mind regularly set on the Spirit and eternity, or your flesh and the world? Why is this the case?

2. How do you renew your mind?

3. How do you find God's will in your life?

4. How did you define love before you read the section on "Understanding True Love?" How does this understanding of love change the way you see things?

Verses to Memorize

Philippians 4:8
Romans 12:1-2
Romans 5:6-8

CHAPTER 5

Understanding Possessions

Now godliness with contentment is great gain.
For we brought nothing into this world, and it
is certain we can carry nothing out. And having
food and clothing, with these we shall be content.

—1 Timothy 6:6-8

It's okay to have wealth. But keep it in your
hands, not in your heart.

—S. Truett Cathy

Vanity of Possessions

You don't have to be a millionaire to be owned by the love of money and think that happiness derives from possessions. You don't have to be in a prison cell to feel locked up in your mind. You don't have to be paranoid to run from the reality of your need for a Savior. You don't have to be homeless to feel lost in this world. And you don't have to be a genius to understand the true meaning of life. So what is the secret to enjoying life, if it doesn't stem from material possessions? Why do so many people live their lives in despair, feeling consumed by emptiness, anger, frustration, and discouragement? As aforementioned, a wise King named Solomon, who lived 3,000 years ago, wrestled with and wrote about this same weighty issue—the meaning of life. Interestingly enough, his words sound a lot like someone in the 21st century who is struggling with the same daunting realities.

Throughout the book of Ecclesiastes, Solomon describes chasing fulfillment in life, saying, "Indeed all was vanity and grasping for the wind" (Ecclesiastes 2:11). There are three unsatisfying areas for living that Solomon extensively tried to find satisfaction in: learning, laboring, and loving. He failed in his quest until he drew conclusions about living a truly satisfying life.

Learning

In biblical times, the name Solomon actually meant wisdom. The man was a wise dude, and no one before or after him possessed such vast wisdom.[165] In his wisdom, King Solomon wrote over 1,000 songs and spoke 3,000 proverbs.[166] He had enough knowledge to lecture others about livestock, fish, and even trees.[167] Groups of people traveled from far places just to listen to his discourses.[168] However, in all his wisdom, Solomon saw that what mattered was being connected to God. This is why he despaired when he perceived the reality of death, for both the wise man and the fool will perish. Death is universal. He reflected in his heart, "As it [death] happens to the fool, it also happens to me [the wise man], and why was I then more wise?" (Ecclesiastes 2:15) So then, what's the point of wisdom? The answer is, there is no point, without God.

Solomon never said that knowledge and wisdom were worthless; he merely explored the importance of putting wisdom in its proper place. He said, "Then I saw that wisdom excels folly as light excels darkness. The wise man's eyes are in his head, but the fool walks

---

165 1 Kings 3:7-12, 4:30, 10:1-8
166 1 Kings 4:32
167 I Kings 4:33
168 1 Kings 10:24

in darkness. Yet I myself perceived that the same event happens to them all" (Ecclesiastes 2:13-14). Moreover, he saw that knowledge, in and of itself, could not bring fulfillment in life. While knowledge of life (psychology, biology, neurology…etc.) can describe life, it cannot explain the reason for life. This knowledge cannot offer morality or values.

Consider sexually transmitted diseases. While we understand and *know* what causes them, we cannot ultimately *stop* sexually transmitted diseases, unless we act within the moral framework that God provides in regards to sex. There are reasons why God has reserved the glorious act of sex between a man and his wife in the context of marriage.[169] There must be balance—we should seek knowledge, but not worship it. Furthermore, filling our brains with facts about life will never satisfy our heart's deepest desires. In other words, knowledge is not an end but a means to explaining life.

The reality is that wisdom comes from God through trials. According to Scripture, wisdom is exercising justice, and fearing and knowing God.[170] When trials come, we usually wonder why. Much like Job, every time I've asked *why* out of bitterness or anger, God has humbled me by showing me a greater

---

[169] See Genesis 2:24; 1 Corinthians 7:2; Hebrews 13:4
[170] Proverbs 1:7

purpose for the trial I was experiencing. This brings about godly fear and humility in my life. Consider this proverb from King Solomon:

> "My son, if you receive my words,
> And treasure my commands within you,
> So that you incline your ear to wisdom,
> And apply your heart to understanding;
> Yes, if you cry out for discernment,
> And lift up your voice for understanding,
> If you seek her as silver,
> And search for her as for hidden treasures;
> Then you will understand the fear of the Lord,
> And find the knowledge of God.
> For the Lord gives wisdom;
> From His mouth come knowledge and understanding;
> He stores up sound wisdom for the upright;
> He is a shield to those who walk uprightly;
> He guards the paths of justice,
> And preserves the way of His saints.
> Then you will understand righteousness and justice,
> Equity and every good path.
>
> When wisdom enters your heart,
> And knowledge is pleasant to your soul,
> Discretion will preserve you;
> Understanding will keep you" (Proverbs 2:1-11).

Laboring

"Therefore I hated life because the work that was done under the sun was distressing to me, for all is vanity and grasping for the wind. Then I hated all my labor in which I had toiled under the sun, because I must leave it to the man who will come after me" (Ecclesiastes 2:17-18).

When our achievements determine our identity, we will eventually feel empty and let down because we are trying to find our satisfaction in things "under the sun" apart from the joy that God gives us in Him. At some point, we reach exhaustion from the endless cycle of work. A businessman will be let down when he is passed up for a promotion that he deserved. A farmer will be disappointed when his crops are destroyed from a flood. A mother of young children will feel defeated when a room in the house looks like a tornado hit it, three seconds after she cleaned it. A young man may feel it is pointless to pursue marriage because he doesn't want his heart broken. Many times we feel like Solomon when he said, "For what has man for all his labor, and for the striving of his heart with which he has toiled under the sun? For all his days are sorrowful, and his work burdensome; even in the night his heart takes no rest. This also is vanity" (Ecclesiastes 2:22-23).

Despair is the result of finding our identity in things. Why? Those who love the things of this world will not be satisfied with them.[171] Moreover, possessions (as a result of our work) can keep us from rest and bring us

---

[171] Ecclesiastes 5:10

grief as they do not last beyond this momentary life we live.[172] So what should we do with work?

We know that God gives us the ability to work, and that a person's portion in life is to labor and enjoy the fruit of their labor. The question you have to ask yourself is *do my possessions possess me?* If they have a hold on your life, you will feel empty and unsatisfied in your labor. If your possessions are not controlling you, God will give you joy in your labor, your perspective will change, and your heart will be content in simplistic living. Fulfillment in our work is futile without God at the center of it.

Loving

God instituted marriage as the fundamental expression of personal love that a man can have with his wife. Solomon promoted marriage but knew that relationships were not going to give anyone complete satisfaction in their life.[173] Jesus echoed Solomon's words by telling us that even marriage is temporary.[174] Of all people, Solomon, through his experience (he had hundreds of wives and concubines) knew that

---

[172] Ecclesiastes 5:12-17

[173] Ecclesiastes 9:9

[174] Matthew 22:30

companionship through marriage would not satisfy his heart's deepest needs.

While relationships will never gratify our vast longings for companionship, the gift of God in a relationship will bring us joy.[175] Friendships hold value but apart from God, they are meaningless, for God is our fundamental companion.[176] While love for others is a noble thing, we will surely be grasping at the wind if we forget our first love, and neglect our love for God—for this is the greatest commandment.[177]

A Life worth Living: Wisdom, Fear, and Obedience

As Solomon tried to attain this satisfying life through possessions and other people, he came to the conclusion that life apart from God was truly meaningless. Again, in regard to our mindset on possessions, we should enjoy them, but not be possessed by them.

There are instances where God may give us possessions but *not* the ability to enjoy them.[178] In contrast, He may give us possessions *and* the ability

---

[175] See Ecclesiastes 4:9-16

[176] John 15:15

[177] Revelation 2:4; Matthew 22:37-38

[178] See Ecclesiastes 6:1-2

to enjoy them.[179] Furthermore, He may give us possessions but then, through trials, take them all away.[180] He may call us to a life of material poverty, riches, or somewhere in between.[181] And as we saw with the rich young ruler, God may allow us to become wealthy but then call us to voluntary poverty in order to show others that He is our greatest treasure.[182] In whatever material life we have, our response should be to enjoy our possessions by putting them in the right place, always remembering that every good and perfect gift comes from Him.[183] Therefore, we stand on Jesus' promise that we do, in fact, feel a greater blessing when we give rather than receive.[184]

Toward the end of his life, King Solomon found the secret to the "good life" and he summed up his book by saying, "Let us hear the conclusion of the whole matter: Fear God and keep His commandments, for this is man's all. For God will bring every work into judgment, including every secret thing, whether good or evil" (Ecclesiastes 12:13-14). Without God, we have nothing. We need Him every second of every day. So, we fear Him for He is holy, and we are not.

---

[179] See Proverbs 10:22; Ecclesiastes 5:19

[180] See Hebrews 10:34

[181] See 2 Chronicles 32:29; Proverbs 30:8; 2 Corinthians 6:10, 8:9

[182] See Matthew 19:21; Mark 10:21; Luke 18:22

[183] James 1:17

[184] Acts 20:35

The Hebrew word for fear is *yârê* which means piety and reverence. The first time the word is used in Scripture is when God tells Abraham, "Now I know that you fear God, since you have not withheld your son, your only son, from Me" (Genesis 22:12). Abraham feared God and obeyed Him when God tested his faith. Faith is what saved him.[185] Faith is what saves us if we believe in the One from whom things are accomplished.[186]

We see from Scripture that we are called to a life of wisdom in Christ who gives us a healthy fear and fuels us toward a right relationship with God. A person's fear of the Lord leads to wisdom and obedience.[187] This wisdom helps our response to difficult times. We should rejoice when God prospers us and reflect when adversity comes, because we know that God is sovereign over all.[188] Our fear of Him leads us to repentance and obedience—this is truly how we express our love for Him.[189] Pretending to live life without God is foolish. Living a life of selfishness is mundane and meaningless. When we try to gain the world, it profits nothing, and we forfeit our souls.[190] Without God, life is nothing but a grasp for the wind.

---

[185] Genesis 15:6

[186] John 15:5

[187] Proverbs 1:7

[188] Ecclesiastes 7:14; Job 1:21; Ecclesiastes 5:15

[189] See 1 John 5:1-5

[190] Matthew 16:26

Testimony – Sacrificial Surrender

I often wonder why there are so many examples in Scripture where people were called or led to give everything they owned in order to further the kingdom of God. Consider the account of the widow who gave all that she had. Jesus said, "Truly I say to you that this poor widow has put in more than all; for all these out of their abundance have put in offerings for God, but she out of her poverty put in all the livelihood that she had" (Luke 21:3-4).

I met a young man (we'll call him Gatimu) in the rural part of the Rift Valley in Kenya. He was catching small fish for his family when our paths crossed. He carried his bundle of fish (soon to be his family's dinner) on a big stick. A group of children passed him by and, without hesitation, he gave each child a fish to take home. At first I thought Gatimu was their father or relative. However, I soon realized that they were strangers. Gatimu gave up his big catch for the day to a group of children who he never met because, as he put it, "it feels better to give things away than to receive them."

I learned something from Gatimu that day. He showed me that giving sacrificially is never a burden, when we daily receive an endless supply of love from the One who provides all things.

Questions for Reflection

1. Do your possessions possess you? If so, how can you change this?

2. Do you understand the reality of the meaninglessness of seeking after things (learning, laboring, and loving) without the joy of God?

3. Do you live a life with a sense of freedom from earthly pleasures?

Verses to Memorize

Ecclesiastes 12:13-14
1 Timothy 6:6-8
Proverbs 1:7

CHAPTER 6

True Stewardship

Therefore do not worry, saying, 'What shall we eat?' or 'What shall we drink?' or 'What shall we wear?' For after all these things the Gentiles seek. For your heavenly Father knows that you need all these things. But seek first the kingdom of God and His righteousness, and all these things shall be added to you. Therefore do not worry about tomorrow, for tomorrow will worry about its own things. Sufficient for the day is its own trouble.

—Matthew 6:31-34

There cannot be a surer rule, nor a stronger exhortation to the observance of it, than when we are taught that all the endowments which we possess are divine deposits entrusted to us for the very purpose of being distributed for the good of our neighbor.

—John Calvin

Stewardship Defined

While in Huruma Village, I was told by my Kenyan father and mother not to give a "handout" to any of the villagers—especially if they asked for one. In other words, I was advised to refrain from simply giving one of the villagers money without first building a relationship with them. I will discuss this advice in further detail in a later chapter, but for now, I want to let you know that the wisdom behind the guidance was centered on the idea of stewardship. So what exactly is stewardship, and how is stewardship connected to suffering?

In the New Testament books, two Greek words express the meaning of the word "stewardship" in the English language. The first word is *epitropos*, which is derived from the word "steward" to mean "foreman, manager, treasurer, or overseer." The second word is *oikonomos,* which similarly means "steward, administrator, or overseer." This second Greek word occurs more frequently in the New Testament and it often refers to the law or management of a household and its affairs or possessions.

Let me suggest to you that a person's material worth only matters if they bear fruit of sanctification and holiness. We are called to be faithful stewards. Our faithfulness to this calling magnifies God's grace and provision in our lives. And while we tend to equate the word stewardship with managing finances and balancing budgets, Scripture gives us various ways God has called us to steward outside of the monetary realm.

Stewarding Time

You will spend every second until you are called home. Time is constant. With *money*, you have the ability to choose how much to give, spend, and save. With *time*, you will spend every last second of the time you have been given, here on Earth. Time is a gift. Time doesn't hold any value unless it is used.

While studying the concept of stewarding time in the Scriptures, I was shocked to find very few passages that directly addressed the issue compared to, say, stewarding our money or treasures. I wanted to include this section because, as an American, I know that the Western society places more of an emphasis on time. As a brother from South America once told me, "The Americans' clock runs and ours walks."

Westerners tend to see time as a resource and forget that time *does not* equate to money. Time cannot be accumulated or saved. At a fixed rate of 60 seconds per minute, every person in history is forced to "spend" his or her time. The problem we face is not how much time God has given us, but how we view and use it for His purposes. Like Paul said, "whatever you do, do all to the glory of God" (1 Corinthians 10:31b). God is not limited by time, but we are.[191] As Robert Banks said back in 1983, which proves even more relevant today:

"Our encounters with others are becoming more and more limited and instrumental. We associate rather than interrelate, hold ourselves back rather than open ourselves up, pass on or steal by one another rather than pause and linger awhile. The number of our close friends drops and the quality of our married life diminishes."[192]

The word "time" in the English language is actually translated two ways in the Greek. The Greek word *kairos* (which is used 30 times by Paul in the New Testament) describes a *definite* or *fixed* time that refers to a particular event. For example a "time of opportunity," a "difficult time," or the "fullness of time."[193] In contrast, the word *chronos* refers to an elapsed or duration of time. *Chronos* is what we are called to steward in our daily lives.

Rather than looking at your schedule and proposing ways to use the time you have been given, the key is not taking time for granted. We steward

---

[191] 1 Timothy 1:17; Hebrews 11:3; 2 Peter 3:8

[192] Robert Banks, *The Tyranny of Time: When 24 Hours Is Not Enough*, InterVarsity, Downers Grove, IL, 1983, p. 51

[193] See Ephesians 5:15-17; Galatians 6:10

our time by first realizing that our time here on Earth is a gift. The sheer frailty of human life should bring us to careful consideration of how we number our days by stewarding our time.[194] When we do so, we understand that slothful hands bring poverty and can result in physical suffering to include hunger.[195]

The Danger of Busyness

On the other hand, while we have to understand that our limited time on Earth holds eternal ramification, we must be careful to understand the dangers of falling into a mentality that perceives time strictly from a functional viewpoint, where performance (our works) is the definitive goal. When we view time in this utilitarian way, we lose the ability to simply sit still and enjoy God and His creation.[196] Clearly, stewarding our time does not and should not, equate to busyness.

First, we must be aware that many of us will subconsciously fill our schedules with things to do in order to bolster our prideful or egocentric hearts. An example of this, could be scheduling meetings and appointments for the sole purpose of showing

---

[194] Psalm 90:12

[195] Proverbs 10:4, 19:15, 20:4, 13

[196] Psalm 46:10

off how important or successful we are in life. Again, this is, at times, subconsciously accomplished as pride continues to warrant busyness.

Secondly, we must realize that our individual and unique priorities (that line up with God's will) should determine how we spend our time, and not cater solely to the desires of others. This is not to say that we become selfish with our time. Rather, we should beware of the sinful tendency to please people rather than God. A clear biblical example of this is when the disciples gathered together other believers and delegated some of the daily tasks in order to continue in what they were led to do in the moment—mainly prayer and preaching the Word publicly.[197] The prioritization of our time must be operated within the framework of our prioritization of our lives and values that are grounded in the truth in God's Word.

In addition, we must acknowledge that there is a temptation to use busyness to satisfy our greed. Each year we seem to take on more and more responsibility in order to pursue riches for the sake of accumulating material wealth. This greed can also stem from a desire for more power, prestige, or even security. Our busyness in this case is a result of our priorities being

---

[197] Acts 6:1-7

misplaced. It is important to remind ourselves of what Jesus said,

> "Do not lay up for yourselves treasures on earth, where moth and rust destroy and where thieves break in and steal; but lay up for yourselves treasures in heaven, where neither moth nor rust destroys and where thieves do not break in and steal. For where your treasure is, there your heart will be also." (Matthew 6:19-21).

Furthermore, we must be aware that our busyness may just be a cover up for laziness. Sometimes we fill our schedules in order to avoid taking on the more important or difficult tasks and responsibilities. Take relationships, for example. Rather than taking the time and emotional energy to sit down and work through a conflict, we instead avoid the difficult discussions by doing something else we conveniently deem as more "important."

Lastly, consider the phrase, "I just don't have enough time to…" Raise your hand if you have ever said (or thought about saying) this phrase? Okay, you can put your hands down now. Busyness has plagued our lives. Everyone always seems to be busy all the time. It is easy for us to excuse busyness as diligence. We essentially put a mask on busyness and use it as a way to make ourselves and others think that our self-worth is unmatched. Rather than slow down and get alone with God in silence,[198] we would rather fill our days with activity as a way of avoiding responsibility. Remember, Jesus rebuked Martha when he told her not to be "worried and troubled about many things" (Luke 10:41).

So do we really trust that God will give us enough time to accomplish what He has called us to accomplish moment by moment? In the end, time is invaluable if we understand how we are called to steward it. Since no time is promised to any of us, may God teach us to number our days by making them count.[199]

Stewarding Talents

According to Scripture, God has given Christians unique gifts for the purpose of glorifying Him and serving others.[200] These gifts are never to be neglected but rather used in various situations.[201] We are commanded to steward our gifts in such a way that serves and ministers to others.[202] The apostle Peter organizes spiritual gifts into two categories. One is

---

[198] Mark 1:35

[199] Psalm 90:12

[200] See Romans 12:3-8; Ephesians 2:19-22; 1 Peter 4:10-11; 2 Timothy 1:6

[201] 1 Timothy 4:14

[202] 1 Peter 4:10

speaking which includes teaching, exhortation, and encouragement. The other is serving, which includes giving, showing compassion, and mercy.

It is important that we understand that those who use the gift of speech whether written or verbal, should keep their words rooted in the Truth of God's Word because, "All Scripture is given by inspiration of God, and is profitable for doctrine, for reproof, for correction, for instruction in righteousness, that the man of God may be complete, thoroughly equipped for every good work" (2 Timothy 3:16-17). On the other hand, those who serve should do so through God's strength—not their own, because Jesus is the Vine, and we are the branches and without Him, we can do nothing.[203] Moreover, we are who we are only because of God's grace toward us.[204]

Each day we have a choice in the way we use our talents. Our sinful nature wants to forward our own agenda and feed our inner pride. However, God has called us to use the talents that *He* has given us for His greater purposes. We are called to serve, "for even the Son of Man [Jesus] did not come to be served, [even though He had every right] but to serve, and to give His life [on the cross] a ransom for many" (Mark

---

[203] John 15:4-5
[204] 1 Corinthians 15:10; Colossians 1:29

10:45). Ponder that astonishing truth before you read the next section!

Stewarding Treasures

God doesn't seek our treasures, but our hearts. Jesus rebuked those who honored Him with their tithes, but had hearts and desires rooted in pride.[205] Consider this. In any relationship, we desire to be loved by simply being in a person's presence and spending time with them. How many children have expressed (sometimes non-verbally) to their fathers, "Daddy, I don't want your gifts. I just want to spend time with you"?

While we can't serve God *and* money[206] we can serve God *with* money. According to Scripture, our attitude toward our money should be one of joy and generosity. We should all give according to and beyond our means.[207] We know that God is always able to provide in abundance what we need in order to accomplish the work He has given us.[208]

As stewards of His treasures, it is important to understand the balance between resting in God's provision and our obligation to work hard in order

---

[205] Matthew 15:8, 23:23

[206] Matthew 6:24

[207] 2 Corinthians 8:3

[208] 2 Corinthians 9:8

to gain. Scripture discussed both. On one hand, we know that God will provide, "Look at the birds of the air, for they neither sow nor reap nor gather into barns; yet the heavenly Father feeds them. Are you not more value than they" (Matthew 6:26)? However, this does not mean we are to sit idly and expect that food and clothing will rain down from heaven. Remember, mankind was given the task to work before sin even entered the world.[209] Moreover, we ought to be wary that we don't take for granted God's provision and squander His gifts away.[210]

On the other hand, we are called to work and provide for ourselves and our families. Those who do not provide for their own household because of idleness have "denied the faith and [are] worse than an unbeliever" (1 Timothy 5:8). So in one sense we are commanded to work and provide. At the same time, we are called to trust. We can trust God that as we faithfully and diligently work to provide for the needs of ourselves and our loved ones, He will take care of His children. Sadly, when we don't consider the whole counsel of God found in Scripture, we develop unbiblical views toward faith and work.

---

[209] God gave Adam the task of tending and keeping the garden before sin entered the world. After the fall of man, work became difficult (See Genesis 3:17-19).

[210] See Luke 15:11-32 and Proverbs 21:20 for examples

These false religions and beliefs plague the church and deceive so many into an unbiblical view of life.[211]

Our motives to gain treasures should also stem from a heart of giving. As Paul said, "Let him who stole steal no longer, but rather let him labor, working with his hands what is good, that he may have something to give him who has need" (Ephesians 4:28). In other words, we have a choice. We can either steal to gain, work to gain, or work to gain *in order to give.* The latter is clearly the biblical stance.

Scripture also makes clear that God is after our motives and hearts. Repeatedly, He probes us to ask not how much we should *give* but rather how much we should *keep* in order to provide for our needs, for if we have merely food and clothing, we will be content.[212] All is His and so we would be wise to seek Him in how we steward the temporary treasures He has given us.[213] As Jesus said, if we are not faithful in the stewardship of our earthly treasures, how can God trust us to steward true, eternal riches?[214]

---

[211] The Word of Faith movement is extremely destructive and unbiblical. See https://gotquestions.org/Word-Faith.html for a good summary of the heretical teaching.

[212] 1 Timothy 6:8

[213] Psalm 24:1

[214] Luke 16:11

Giving an Account

A study of God's design for stewarding our possessions reinforces the reality of God's ownership and our responsibility. Matthew 25:14-46 is a great passage to contemplate. We are clearly stewards of His property. Our aim is not to find out what to do with our possessions, but rather find out what the Owner wants us to do with what He has given us.

A correct mindset in this area of our lives is monumental, for all of us will give an account to God for what He has entrusted to us during our lifetime. Moreover, this biblical thinking helps us combat greed and materialism. The Word of God is a weapon, and we would do well to use it to fight the sin of loving the creation rather than our Creator.

Stewarding Relationships

Since the fall of man, relationships have been broken and in desperate need of radical healing.[215] Our vertical relationship with our heavenly Father was shattered because of our sinful rebellion. Moreover, every one of our horizontal relationships with mankind also became marred.

Ultimately, we steward our relationships by

---

[215] See Genesis 3

following Jesus' command to treat others in the same way that we desire to be treated.[216] As Christians, our indisputable witness to the world is our love for other people. When Jesus was on Earth in the flesh, He gave us a commandment to love one another in the same sacrificial way that He loved us: "By this all will know that you are My disciples, if you have love for one another" (John 13:35). The relationships we cultivate reflect the way we honor the Lord. If we fail to take ownership and responsibility for the human relationships that God has placed in our life, we will fail to show the world the truest and purest definition of love—God Himself.[217]

One point of emphasis: be wary if your friendships or relationships are not causing sanctifying wounds.[218] Those who love you need to be willing to hold you accountable and even "wound" your pride in order for you to grow in spiritual maturity. We all need friends to encourage us,[219] but we also need friends who are willing to use the Word (the truth) to lovingly spur us toward holiness in Christ.[220]

Take a moment now to reflect on the relationships you have around you. Consider evaluating yourself in

---

[216] Matthew 7:12; Luke 6:31

[217] 1 John 4:7-8

[218] Proverbs 27:6

[219] 1 Thessalonians 5:11; 1 John 3:18

[220] Psalm 141:5

the area of stewardship. We all have eyes watching us as we live our lives. Are you setting a noble example for them as they observe the way you speak, react, and love? The reality is that you will teach them *something* even if you teach them *nothing*. For me, that's really the definition of parenting. As the group *Phillips, Craig, and Dean* sing in reference to being fathers to their respective sons:

> "Lord, I want to be just like You
> 'Cause he wants to be just like me
> I want to be a holy example
> For his innocent eyes to see
> Help me be a living Bible, Lord
> That my little boy can read
> I want to be just like You
> 'Cause he wants to be like me."

Stewarding Body

Stewarding our bodies extends beyond physical exercise. While physical strength or growth is important,[221] we should be more concerned with our eternal being. While bodily exercise profits some, godliness is profitable for all things.[222] When we see our bodies as our own, we will either worship them (a real struggle in Western cultures) or neglect them.

---

[221] Luke 2:52; 1 Samuel 2:26

[222] 1 Timothy 4:8

However, when we as Christians see our bodies as God's temple, bought at a high price[223]—namely Jesus' death on the cross—we will have a better understanding of how to apply Paul's exhortation when he said, "Therefore, whether you eat or drink, or whatever you do, do all to the glory of God" (1 Corinthians 10:31).

We can sin with almost every part of our body. Our eyes can covet and lust, our hands can hurt, and our hearts and minds can dishonor God. As part of stewarding our bodies, we must be cognizant of the reality of our sin. But take heart, because we fight the sin of our bodies with the sword of the Spirit.[224] This sword is the Word of God (the Bible) and is *sharper* than a two-edged sword.[225] While we see in Proverbs that lust is tasteful like honey and momentarily pleasing, it is bitter in the end and leads to death because it is sharp as a two-edged sword.[226] But, the Word of God is not only living and active, but *sharper* and *stronger* than a two-edged sword![227] If we believe the truth that we find in Scripture, our bodies must only be used for God's purposes and glory.

---

[223] 1 Corinthians 3:9, 6:19-20

[224] Ephesians 6:17

[225] Hebrews 4:12

[226] Proverbs 5:3-5

[227] Hebrews 4:12

Stewards of the Gospel

As Christians, we are entrusted to be good stewards of the gospel of Jesus Christ[228] as we make disciples and teach others about the Truth that sets us free.[229] While we are called to diligently preach the Word to all,[230] the burden is absent as the gospel liberates us from feeling unequipped. The gospel compels us to loosen our grip on the things of this temporary world, by giving us a heart to see people as sheep who need their Shepherd. As Jesus said, "I am the good shepherd. The good shepherd gives His life for the sheep" (John 10:11).

Jesus' Example

When was the last time you felt stressed because you didn't accomplish what you had planned? Have you ever felt frustrated or guilty because you thought you were a failure? Is the answer to organize your life? Maybe, at the same time, there will always be more needs that arise. While in Huruma Village, I felt like there was never enough time to accomplish what I wanted to accomplish. I think God was teaching me

---

[228] 1 Corinthians 9:17

[229] John 8:32

[230] 2 Timothy 4:2

patience (yet again) and to trust in His sovereignty and rest on His promises, timing, and perfect will.

Consider this, Jesus Christ completed His ministry on Earth in three years, and yet He never once even appeared to be in a rush. While the gospels document that Jesus was incredibly "busy" even to the point of physical exhaustion, He always seemed to have time to minister and love those He was around.[231] Is it not marvelous that Jesus is able to sympathize with us in our weaknesses?[232]

Jesus cared about the people and their needs. His compassion fueled His work to heal the sick, comfort the grieving, and save the lost. His life was never characterized by a sense of worry or stress over time. Jesus, the only perfect steward, gave up all He had and died to give us life.[233] When we fail to steward well, we suffer physically, emotionally, mentally, psychologically, and spiritually. However, when we look to our Savior, we see that true stewardship brings us hope and alleviates unnecessary suffering.

---

[231] See John 4:1-26

[232] Hebrews 4:15

[233] Philippians 2:6-8

A Father's Gift

When my daughter was 18 months old, she took a plastic bag of raisins off of our kitchen counter. I asked if I could have one, and she replied in a rather strong tone of voice, "No! Mine!" I pondered the situation for a moment and then wondered, "In what sense were they ever hers?" The reality is that she was totally dependent on me to even open the bag. Furthermore, she was dependent on me to work in order to provide. Clearly, the raisins were not hers.

How often do we act the same way toward God who provides us all things? How many times during the day do we go into "toddler mode" and say, "This is my time, my talent, my treasures, me relationship, and my body!" An unbiblical and thereby sinful outlook and attitude toward the gifts that God has given us, will inevitably corrupt our life. These gifts are not about us, as we are called to worship the Giver, not the gifts.[234]

I appreciate C.S. Lewis' perspective on stewardship when he said, "Nothing that you have not given away will be really yours." Do you believe this truth?

---

[234] See Romans 1:18-25

Testimony – All for Him

Okapi Wajuri grew up in a Kenyan slum. He has no recollection of his parents because he was dumped in a garbage disposal as an infant. His first memories consist of begging for food while walking the streets of Nairobi. One Sunday, Okapi passed by a church where he heard people worshipping God through song. On that day, God grabbed Okapi's heart and gave him a desire to seek the Truth. Knowing Jesus became Okapi's aim and motivation in his life.

After saving up his money for four months, Okapi purchased his first Bible. He read it every single day and soon discovered the relational God who loved him. This young Kenyan knew that Jesus could relate to his pain because He too suffered. Okapi's heart radically changed as he worshipped the One who was "despised and rejected by man, a man of sorrows [suffering], and acquainted [familiar] with grief [pain]" (Isaiah 53:3). God understands suffering because He chose to experience it when He sent His Son to us.

Okapi found ultimate healing by trusting in Jesus—the One who gave His life so that we may live. Okapi found the Savior in the midst of His suffering; it was there that this personal relationship was strengthened and understood.

"But He was wounded for our transgressions,
He was bruised for our iniquities;
The chastisement for our peace was upon Him,
And by His stripes we are healed" (Isaiah 53:5).

Questions for Reflection

1. What area of stewardship do you most struggle with in your life right now? Why?

2. Write out your weekly schedule. Are you subject to an unhealthy amount of busyness?

3. What are the priorities in your life? Why? Write them down and share them with someone you trust.

Verses to Memorize

1 Corinthians 10:31
Romans 12:1-2
Psalm 90:12

CHAPTER 7

An Outlook on Poverty

Open your mouth for the speechless, in the cause of all who are appointed to die. Open your mouth, judge righteously, and plead the cause of the poor and needy.

—Proverbs 31:8-9

Poverty is rooted in broken relationships, so the solution to poverty is rooted in the power of Jesus' death and resurrection to put all things in right relationship again.

—Brian Fikkert

The Reality of Poverty

In 2016, the United Nations and World Bank estimated that 1.5 billion people live in absolute poverty. These statistics show that twenty percent of the world's population falls within this category and three-quarters of the overall population live on less than $2 per day which is $730 per year.[235] Moreover, conservative statistics show that over 26,000 children *today* will die due to either starvation or a *preventable* disease.[236]

Our world is filled with various types of injustice. Along with severe poverty, there is an estimated 153 million orphans,[237] 27 million living in slavery, and over 45 million babies who are murdered in their mother's womb each year. Basic math shows us that 125,000 children are murdered each day![238] We are told to "Defend the poor and the fatherless; do justice to the afflicted and needy" (Psalm 82:3). What are we missing? Have we turned a blind eye or a deaf ear to these realities?

---

[235] http://povertydata.worldbank.org/poverty/home/. Accessed November 2016.

[236] World Bank. 2015. Poverty website. www.worldbank.org/en/topic/poverty and the Overview page www.worldbank.org/en/topic/poverty/overview Accessed November 2016.

[237] Statistics from the United Nations Children's Fund (UNICEF)

[238] Statistics from the World Health Organization (WHO)

What is Poverty?

While there are a plethora of organizations around the world that involve themselves in alleviating poverty, I'm afraid that few understand how to effectively combat it because they don't fully grasp the true reality. North American's observation of poverty is simply a lack of material things (primarily money), and so they believe the solution is to provide material things to those who are characterized as "poor" within their communities.

According to the Oxford Dictionary, an individual is poor when he or she lacks sufficient money to live at a standard considered comfortable or normal in a society. Moreover, the Census Bureau categorizes poverty when, "a family's total income is less than the family's threshold, then that family and every individual in it is considered in poverty."[239] These materialistic definitions of poverty are concerning because an individual's "comfortableness in society" or "threshold income", varies depending on the society or the social-economic part of the world that surrounds them. An individual's standard of living is clearly skewed in wealthier cultures.

Furthermore, these definitions can be harmful because an absence of material things is merely a

[239] See https://www.census.gov/topics/income-poverty/poverty/guidance/poverty-measures.html

symptom of poverty. From a medical standpoint, when a doctor continues to treat a patient's symptoms rather than the underlying causes, the disease never resides and could continue to worsen. This is true when those who fight poverty simply "throw money" at the situation. There are too many to list, but many programs around the world fail to put a dent in the war on poverty because they see poverty as simply a lack of money.

Authors Steven Corbett and Brian Filkkert understand this problem and educate churches on the reality of poverty alleviation. Part of their research cited a 2000 study conducted by World Bank who interviewed 60,000 people worldwide and asked them to define poverty. When asked what it means to be "poor," 90% of the people interviewed used psychological, emotional, spiritual, and social terms. Rather than describing their lack of material needs (such as water, clothes, food…etc.) they used phrases such as, "To be full of shame, less than human, a lack of dignity, feeling inferior, and embarrassment."

The testimonial research clearly redefines poverty as broken relationships within social, psychological, and spiritual realms. With that, a holistic approach to poverty alleviation must be considered. While I agree that people around the world are starving, they are ultimately starving of healthy relationships.

Relationships Matter

With God

The world functions around relationships. As a child of God, we are told to call Him "our Father" because He is more than just our Creator and Judge. As a Christian, I have been adopted into God's family and therefore, can cry to Him, "Abba, Father." This picture that the apostle Paul paints for us in Romans 8:14-17 is one of a little child crying out, "Daddy, Daddy!" When we reject God's authority in our life or see Him as irrelevant, our relationship with Him is marred, which will lead us to a path of poverty on a social, psychological, and spiritual stage.

With Self

Along with our relationship with God, our relationship with ourselves is imperative. We should look through the lens of Scripture and believe the truth that we are all uniquely created in God's image. Our identity should be found in Christ, which will help us avoid becoming prideful and feeling a sense of superiority. At the same time, this identity will help give us confidence knowing that God loved us so much that He was willing to die for us, so that we may live. I'm convinced that a marred or broken self-identity is the reason the United States alone reports over 40,000 *confirmed* suicides a *year*, and an estimated suicide *attempt* every thirty one *seconds*.[240]

With Others

Furthermore, our relationships with others also matter, and are easily tainted because of our tendencies to become dependent and independent. These two unconscious relationship behaviors make it difficult to foster long-term, healthy relationships with others because they are rooted in self-centeredness. Dependent relationships cause us to determine or condition our thinking that we can accomplish our goals or "go through life" by depending on others to carry the load. On the other hand, independent relationships are derived from a prideful and selfish attitude that is praised in Western cultures, as those who are independent, are seen as "strong."

However, biblically, we see are called to be *interdependent* in our relationships with others. It's the balance of holding ourselves accountable for our actions[241] and responsibilities, but being willing to lean on others for support. This balance is not

---

[240] American Association of Suicidology, www.suicidology.org/Portals/14/docs/Resources/FactSheets/2012datapgsvid.pdf, Accessed October 2016.

[241] See Romans 14:12; Galatians 6:1-5

a contradiction for we are called to "bear our own loads" (Galatians 6:5) and at the same time, "bear one another's burdens" (Galatians 6:2). When we are interdependent, our relationships with others flourish. In relation to poverty, these relationships whether familial or not, give individuals the ability to fight poverty from a holistic approach.

With the World

Finally, our relationship to the world (i.e. creation) comes in the form of stewardship as even before the fall, mankind is called and commanded to have dominion over our God's creation. While the Earth and all of creation is the Lord's,[242] we are to ensure it functions as we care for His creation. The two sinful tendencies in this area are workaholics and slothfulness. When we fail to rely on God's strength to accomplish His will, we toil out of a sense of a healthy pride and feeling of self-worth. While we are called to work hard, we have to understand our limits and priorities. It's the balance between becoming a Martha or a Mary.[243] On the other hand, we can also gravitate towards a lazy attitude which God clearly says is sinful.[244]

---

[242] Psalm 24:1-2

[243] See Luke 10:38-42

[244] See Proverbs 10:4, 12:24, 19:15, 21:25

How Do We Respond to Poverty?

As communities, churches, ministries, organizations—as individual human beings, how do we respond to the poverty epidemic that has taken billions of lives, and crushed them under the weight of neglect and broken relationships? The transformation process may seem impossible to overcome when we contemplate poverty statistics. May I suggest that, as a church, we make the sacrificial effort to care for and build relationships with others? Our care for others will fuel us into taking the actions necessary to fight the war on poverty.

For encouraging purposes, I want you to consider the wisdom literature book of Job. We remember Job as a real, historical figure whom the Bible considered a righteous man.[245] We find explanations of God allowing suffering as a means to sanctify a person. We also see a clear demonstration of God's unfailing love and perfect justice. Despite all of Job's nobility, the one characteristic that God highlighted was his care for the oppressed. While Job was a powerful and influential man, he was revered and honored because he delivered the poor and took care of the widows and orphans.[246] He was intentional with his gifts and

---

[245] Job 1:1
[246] Job 29:11-12

searched out ways to serve those who were oppressed by poverty.[247]

As Christians, we should do the same as God has called us to preach the gospel to the poor, heal the brokenhearted, and bring liberty to those in oppression. In other words, we are commanded to find ways to give and serve.[248] However, we must understand that serving the needy at time entails us asking them for help. Let me explain.

Remember Mutua from the introduction of this book? I asked him how I could help his situation as he was struggling to provide for his family. He was not the only Kenyan who refused to accept monetary offers. Since poverty is a holistic issue, my narrow mindedness caused me to think that only *I* could help him. It never even dawned on me that I could help him by allowing him to help me. The paradox is radical but understanding this reality propels us all to comprehend the complex natures of poverty.

Is this not the Fast I've Chosen for You?

Ultimately, we respond to poverty by building relationships. Journey with me to Kenya once again as I tell you the story of Dennis and Irene Tongoi.

---

[247] Job 29:16

[248] See Luke 4:18

The Tongoi's are Kenyan natives. Irene is the founder of New Dawn Education Centre (NDEC)[249] that was built in Huruma Village.[250] NDEC is a secondary school (i.e. high school) committed to raising up a generation of godly men and women who will become servant leaders and kingdom seekers. Their curriculum is rooted in a biblical worldview and focuses on holistic discipleship.

Irene was first called to serve the people of Huruma in 2003 when she was convicted by God because of her prior rejection of the villagers. She realized that God uses the church as His advocate for people who are broken and hopeless. NDEC became the new beginning where God provided hope for the lost. God used the Tongoi family to bring faith and hope to a people whose relationships with themselves, others, and God was deeply frayed. When I first interviewed Irene in 2011 to understand the story of NDEC, she quoted the prophet Isaiah when he said,

The Spirit of the Lord God is upon Me,
Because the Lord has anointed Me
To preach good tidings to the poor;

---

[249] *Centre* is not misspelled (i.e., it is not supposed to say *center*). This is how they spell the word *center* in old English. Kenya was a British colony and did not gain its independence until December 12, 1963.

[250] See www.newdawnkenya.com for more information on the secondary school in Huruma Village, Kenya.

He has sent Me to heal the brokenhearted,
To proclaim liberty to the captives,
And the opening of the prison to those who are bound
(Isaiah 61:1).

Dearly beloved, we would do well to heed the Word of the Lord:

"Is this not the fast that I have chosen:
To loose the bonds of wickedness,
To undo the heavy burdens,
To let the oppressed go free,
And that you break every yoke?
Is it not to share your bread with the hungry,
And that you bring to your house the poor who are cast out;
When you see the naked, that you cover him" (Isaiah
58:6-7a).

God has not called us to comfortably sit back and turn a blind eye or deaf ear to the needy. He has called us (as a church and individual) to give our lives spreading the good news of Jesus Christ to the lost. He requires us to seek justice, love mercy, and set the oppressed free.[251]

These are My Children

Overwhelming conviction filled my heart. That's the first feeling I had when God confronted me on my worldly mindset toward the poor in the slums in Africa. My conviction came directly from God,

---

[251] Micah 6:8

through His Word in Matthew chapter 22. Here, Jesus summarized all of God's commandments by saying that we should, "Love the Lord your God with all your heart, with all your soul, and with all your mind.' This is the first and greatest commandment. And the second is like it: 'You shall love your neighbor as yourself.' On these two commandments hang all the Law and the Prophets" (Matthew 22:37-40).

The last phrase is what stuck out to me. I have to love my neighbor as myself? If I were living in a slum, how would I want others to treat me? What if my children suffered persecution like millions around the world? What if my family was hungry? If these were *my* children, how I would act? I would do whatever I could to help them. That's when God nailed me right in the heart. It's as if He was saying, "You see Charles, these are My children—and you are My child. What are you doing to help *My* children? When are you going to stop turning a deaf ear and a blind eye to the cries of help from the poor?" I admit, at times it is extremely uncomfortable to reach out and help. We naturally look away when we pass by a homeless person. But if that person was a member of our own family—or our child—would we still look away?

I pray that God will give us the conviction and compassion to act on behalf of the needy. We can't wait! May we understand the real meaning of poverty and respond in such a way that radically changes our mindset and leads us to action in the Spirit of Christ.[252] As an African Christian brother told me, "Charles, we are not responsible for the outcome, but we are responsible to love others like Christ loved us."[253] Dear friends, His love was radical and costly!

Promises to the Poor

In order to fully grasp the biblical mandate we as a church have to care for the poor, we must understand God's unwavering promises to the poor. First, God provides divine *protection*. Consider these biblical texts in the Psalms regarding protecting the poor.

> "For the oppression of the poor, for the sighing of the needy,
> Now I will arise," says the Lord;
> I will set him in the safety for which he yearns." (Psalm 12:5).

> "You shame the counsel of the poor,
> But the Lord is his refuge" (Psalm 14:6).

> "You, O God, provided from Your goodness for the poor" (Psalm 68:10b).

> "For the Lord hears the poor,
> And does not despise His prisoners" (Psalm 69:33).

---

[252] Romans 8:5-8, 13
[253] See Romans 5:8

"Yet He sets the poor on high, far from affliction,
And makes their families like a flock" (Psalm 107:41).

"For He shall stand at the right hand of the poor,
To save him from those who condemn him" (Psalm 109:31).

"I know that the LORD will maintain the cause of the
    afflicted,
And justice for the poor" (Psalm 140:12).

Second, God gives the poor *providence*. God is a strength (literal translation is "a fortress") to the poor and needy in their distress.[254] A precious encouragement is held out to those who are suffering trials as a result of spiritual or physical poverty.

Third, God gives the poor eternal *provision*. As James writes, "Listen, my beloved brethren: Has God not chosen the poor of this world to be rich in faith and heirs of the kingdom which He promised to those who love Him" (James 2:5)? Consider how often riches lead to vice and sin. Yet, those who are poor are in a more favorable state for peace that surpasses knowledge and understanding. God's provision to the poor may not always come in material blessings. However, faith (which is more powerful than worldly favor) will carry an individual to a rich inheritance in God's eternal kingdom.

Finally, God listens to the *prayers* of the poor.

---

[254] Isaiah 25:4

God hears the cries of the poor and will not forsake them.[255] In contrast, "Whoever shuts his ears to the cry of the poor will also cry himself and not be heard" (Proverbs 21:13).

Spiritual Riches

While in eastern Africa, Proverbs 13:7 continued to come to my mind as it reads, "There is one who makes himself rich, yet has nothing; and one who makes himself poor, yet has great riches." The reality is, a person may possess everything physically but have nothing spiritually. I think this is what Jesus meant when He said that a person can "gain the whole world" and yet "lose his soul."[256] I witnessed this same paradox over and over again. I saw people in dire poverty with complete joy in the Lord, and lived with people who possessed nothing physically, but everything spiritually.

Paul emphasized this truth of spiritual riches when he said to the church in Corinth, "For you know the grace of our Lord Jesus Christ, that though He was rich, yet for your sakes He became poor, that you through His poverty might become rich" (2 Corinthians 8:9). Moreover, James affirms that God

---

[255] See Isaiah 41:17

[256] Mark 8:36

has chosen "the poor of this world to be rich in faith and heirs of the kingdom which he promised to those who love Him" (James 2:5).

While the blessings we receive when we are God's children are evident today (forgiveness, no condemnation, gifts of the Spirit, imputed righteousness…etc.), the riches of the glory of our inheritance are fully realized when Christ returns.[257] There will be no more sickness, pain, suffering, sin, or even death.[258] So, we can conclude that losing everything for the kingdom of God is worth it. As Jesus said, "Again, the kingdom of heaven is like treasure hidden in a field, which a man found and hid; and for joy over it he goes and sells all that he has and buys that field" (Matthew 13:44).

Believers all over the world need to be reminded that suffering any loss in this life is our gain, if we suffer it for the sake of knowing and walking with Christ. As the apostle Paul said,

> "But what things were gain to me, these I have counted loss for Christ. Yet indeed I also count all things loss for the excellence of the knowledge of Christ Jesus my Lord, for whom I have suffered the loss of all things, and count them as rubbish, that I may gain Christ" (Philippians 3:7-8).

---

[257] See Romans 14:17; Ephesians 1:18
[258] Revelation 21:4

Henry Martyn articulated the concept of spiritual riches when he said, "If [God] has work for me to do, I cannot die." In other words, Christians are immortal until God determines that they have finished their work. Therefore, the light that we shine in this dark and broken world (see Matthew 5:16) is more important than life.

Testimony – Adopted by the King

Growing up with seven siblings made me appreciate the intrinsic value of a father and mother's role in a child's life. God clearly designed the family as the core of society.

Poverty creates orphans. While in Kenya, I witnessed a young orphan girl around the age of three walk into a neighborhood slum. No one knew where she came from but they knew she was abandoned. A young man who was also an orphan ended up caring for her needs and eventually adopted her. This young man was living in dire poverty, and yet he knew that God had called His church to take care of orphans as a sign of true religion (see James 1:27). This young man told me that this orphan girl was a "mtoto thamani" which means "precious child."

While this young girl was adopted, we must never forget the tangible reality that, as Christians, we have been chosen, rescued, and ultimately adopted by the King of Kings.

> "For you are all sons of God through faith in Christ Jesus. For as many of you as were baptized into Christ have put on Christ. There is neither Jew nor Greek, there is neither slave nor free, there is neither male nor female; for you are all one in Christ Jesus. And if you are Christ's, then you are Abraham's seed, and heirs according to the promise.

Now I say that the heir, as long as he is a child, does not differ at all from a slave, though he is master of all, but is under guardians and stewards until the time appointed by the father. Even so we, when we were children, were in bondage under the elements of the world. But when the fullness of the time had come, God sent forth His Son, born of a woman, born under the law, to redeem those who were under the law, that we might receive the adoption as sons.

And because you are sons, God has sent forth the Spirit of His Son into your hearts, crying out, "Abba, Father!" Therefore you are no longer a slave but a son, and if a son, then an heir of God through Christ" (Galatians 3:26-4:7).

Questions for Reflection

1. Why does an accurate and holistic definition of poverty matter?

2. What are you doing in your life to live simply in order to give more to the poor?

3. How can you get involved in your community, church, and globally to effectively combat the war on poverty?

4. What does it look like in your life to "care for the least of these?" (Matthew 25:40). Write down three specific ways you can obey God in this area.

5. Poverty Resources: chartiynavigator.org, sabainternational.org, globalhungerrelief.com, samaritanspurse.org, vaporinternational.org, compassion.com, chalmers.org,

Verses to Memorize

Proverbs 28:27
Acts 20:35
1 John 3:17

CHAPTER 8

❖ ❖ ❖

Passing the Test

Examine yourselves as to whether you are in the faith. Test yourselves. Do you not know yourselves, that Jesus Christ is in you?—unless indeed you are disqualified.

—2 Corinthians 13:5

But it is doubtless true, and evident from [the] Scriptures, that the essence of all true religion lies in holy love; and that in this divine affection, and an habitual disposition to it, and that light which is the foundation of it, and those things which are the fruits of it, consists the whole of religion.

—Jonathan Edwards

Admonish

Idleness causes our relationship with God to wane. This is why Paul tells believers to admonish and warn one another.[259] We must warn others of the potential of hardening their heart when trials emanate, the reality that a lack of faith leads to sin, which leads to death, and that ungratefulness robs them of their joy in Christ.

Our relationship with Jesus directs our life, so we must be ready to warn one another about anything that threatens that relationship. Faithful, true, and uplifting are the wounds of a friend who admonishes out of love and concern.[260] Without admonishment, we live a life of self-deception. In order to admonish one another, we first have to inspect the fruit.

Inspect the Fruit

When you are at the market or grocery store buying some fruit, do you simply pick up a banana and put it in your bag? You usually take the time to remove it from the shelf and inspect its ripeness. Why? Because you know that fruit may look good on one side and be rotten on the other. In other words,

---

[259] See 1 Thessalonians 5:14
[260] Proverbs 27:6a

the fruit may be deceiving—so too with a person's good works (fruit) in his or her life.

From a spiritual standpoint, a person is only good with God. Apart from Jesus' transforming our lives, we are bad trees who cannot bear good fruit.[261] Apart from a saving faith in Christ, our works are like filthy rags.[262]

From Head to Heart

As knowledge is imparted to our minds, we can choose whether or not to act and move that knowledge eighteen inches down toward our hearts, for "As a man thinks in his heart, so is he" (Proverbs 23:7a). The goal is to transition from *understanding* knowledge and instruction, "Trust in the LORD with all your heart" (Proverbs 3:5) to literal *application* "When I am afraid, I will trust in You" (Psalm 56:3). We accomplish this application step by focusing our mind on things above and not on the things of this world. The battle rages between the opposing forces of our flesh and the Spirit.

The flesh is our human nature. This nature prefers to gain satisfaction from worldly pleasures, and apart from the Spirit of Jesus Christ in us, we are simply

---

[261] Matthew 7:16-18
[262] Isaiah 64:6

slaves to our flesh.[263] Our flesh is hostile and can lead us to sin and death.[264] The apostle Paul contrasts the fruit of the Spirit (love, joy, peace, patience, kindness, goodness, faithfulness, gentleness, and self-control) with the works of the flesh (adultery, fornication, idolatry, hatred, jealousy, selfish ambition, envy, drunkenness...etc.). So, when we walk in the Spirit, we will not fulfill the lustful desires of our sinful flesh.[265] We don't just believe; we walk (i.e. live) as children of the light. We respond to our sinful temptations by choosing Christ, who is unchanging and fully satisfying.[266]

From a practical standpoint, as Christians, we walk in the Spirit by first thinking of the things of the Spirit. We think about things that are noble, lovely, praiseworthy, excellent, pure, and just.[267] We become transformed by renewing our minds to line up with the things of God.[268] This is also how we move from head *knowledge* to heart *actions*.

---

[263] Romans 7:18

[264] Romans 8:13

[265] Galatians 5:16

[266] See Psalm 16:11

[267] Philippians 4:8

[268] Romans 12:2

Do You Love?

Self-love does not mean you have to gain self-esteem. Jesus commands us to love others as ourselves.[269] We naturally love ourselves. We all seek comfort and happiness. In other words, we cherish and care for our own bodies. Paul admonished husbands to love their wives in the same way that Christ loved His church, by giving Himself up for her. He writes, "For no one ever hated his own flesh, but nourishes and cherishes it" (Ephesians 5:29). The challenge is never to love ourselves because we naturally care for our own needs. The challenge is answering the question: do you love others in the same way?

Love is, in fact, an extension of our faith in Jesus. While our faith justifies us before a holy God because of His love, our love and good works follow and affirm that we are born again. Lives characterized by humble repentance demonstrate our walk with Jesus. As the Scriptures say, we are to bear fruit (good deeds) worthy of repentance and prove our repentance with our deeds.[270]

---

[269] Matthew 22:38-39

[270] Matthew 3:8; Acts 26:20

Faith Leads to Works

There is no such thing as a "carnal Christian" who lives a life professing faith in Christ without demonstrating it. Such people may appear to exist, but the Scriptures expose the false claim that a person can be saved, but still live a life in worldliness with no concern or desire for the things of God, or holiness. As aforementioned, Christians should instead, examine themselves to see if they truly are in Christ.[271] One should ask if his life displays an ongoing evidence of sanctification because without it, he will not see the Lord.[272]

Moreover, the fruit in the individual's life should show genuine faith and repentance.[273] This is precisely why Paul said that we are to prove our repentance with our fruit.[274] He echoes this exhortation in his first letter to Timothy saying that a person's spiritual maturity should be "evident to all" (1 Timothy 4:15). Finally, in his letter to the twelve scattered tribes, James devotes almost half of his letter to discussing how a person's fruit demonstrates assurance of his faith and salvation.[275] While Christians are *always*

---

[271] 2 Corinthians 13:5

[272] Hebrews 12:14

[273] Matthew 3:8, 7:16, 20

[274] Acts 26:20

[275] See James 2

saved by grace and faith *alone* (which comes through repentance),[276] is not obedience to God evidence of saving faith? I believe that Jesus was clear on this issue as you read Matthew's gospel account.[277] Saving faith by its nature produces love for God and others.[278]

How Then Do We Bear Good Fruit?

All good comes from faith in God as a Christian is a new creature in Jesus who has new affections and desires for holiness.[279] This faith, which is itself a gift from God, empowers a person to do good for God's glory, the ultimate aim of all mankind.[280] The Westminster Shorter Catechism captures this very truth. For what is the chief end of man? "To glorify God and enjoy Him forever."[281]

Therefore, progressive sanctification in a Christian's life is apparent because God is working to will and act for His good pleasure.[282] No Christian lives a perfectly holy and righteous life since our glorification comes

---

[276] Romans 10:9-10; Ephesians 2:8-10

[277] Matthew 7:13-14, 21

[278] Galatians 5:6

[279] Romans 14:23b; Hebrews 11:6; 2 Corinthians 5:17

[280] 2 Peter 1:1; Acts 3:16; 1 Corinthians 10:31

[281] See Romans 11:36

[282] Philippians 2:13

when God takes us home.[283] Any Christian will tell you that the battle against the sinful flesh is real (see Romans 8:1-8) and that spiritual growth in holiness is a miraculous work of God's grace. Even so, should we not be aware and examine our own faith? We can't ignore the biblical truth that false faith is not only prevalent, but eternally destructive.[284]

Darkness and Light

God is holy. He is distinct and separate from everything else, and His essence and transcendence are like no other. He hates sin and loves the sinner who repents and follows Him. God is preparing a people for Himself. Christ is the groom and the church is the bride, and He is coming for her.[285] As Jesus said, He will "separate the wicked from among the just, and cast them into [hell]" (Matthew 13:49-50). We may be quick to doubt or mistrust God's righteous judgement, and at times question His sovereignty as we have a hard time understanding His thoughts and ways—which are higher than our own.[286]

We all cry for justice when mass shootings, natural disasters, disease, or any sort of "injustice" on earth

---

[283] See Galatians 5:17

[284] See Matthew 7:21-23, 25:41-26; Titus 1:16; James 2:14-26

[285] See Revelation 19:1-9

[286] Isaiah 55:8

transpires. This mindset proves God's Word to be true that we have a conscience that can discern ethic morality. As the apostle Paul wrote:

> "For the wrath of God is revealed from heaven against all ungodliness and unrighteousness of men, who suppress the truth in unrighteousness, because what may be known of God is manifest in them, for God has shown it to them. For since the creation of the world His invisible attributes are clearly seen, being understood by the things that are made, even His eternal power and Godhead, so that they are without excuse, because, although they knew God, they did not glorify Him as God, nor were thankful, but became futile in their thoughts, and their foolish hearts were darkened" (Romans 1:18-21).

Like our Creator, our attitude toward sin should be one of hatred. We should not be indifferent towards sin. All sin: adultery, gossip, lying, evil thought… etc. is offensive to a holy God. In the end, God's vengeance will be displayed upon those who disobey and reject Him.[287] So we have to ask ourselves, are we following Him or running from Him? As Jesus said:

> "He who believes in Him is not condemned; but he who does not believe is condemned already, because he has not believed in the name of the only begotten Son of God. And this is the condemnation, that the light has come into the world, and men loved darkness rather than light, because their deeds were evil. For everyone practicing evil hates the light and does not come to the light, lest his deeds should

---

[287] See Psalm 7:9-17

be exposed. But he who does the truth comes to the light, that his deeds may be clearly seen, that they have been done in God" (John 3:18-21).

Fight the Good Fight

We want to finish well. The human life is like a race, and like Paul, we want to be able to say, "I have fought the good fight, I have finished the race, I have kept the faith" (2 Timothy 4:7). The only way we can truly fight is by embracing the truth that what Christ accomplished on the cross canceled our sin, and laid the foundation for our justification in Him. Christians have been united with Jesus in His death and resurrection.[288]

As a result of our unity in Jesus, we can consider ourselves "dead indeed to sin, but alive to God in Christ Jesus our Lord" (Romans 6:11). This is precisely why we are commanded and empowered to not let sin reign in our lives.[289] This concept of sanctified living is accomplished by what God has done. In the death of Christ, we were bought; we are no longer our own. "Or do you not know that your body is the temple of the Holy Spirit who is in you [indicative], whom you have from God, and you are not your own? For you were bought at a price; therefore glorify God

---

[288] Romans 6:5
[289] Romans 6:12

in your body [imperative] and in your spirit, which are God's" (1 Corinthians 6:19-20). Moreover, in the death of Christ, we are forgiven and therefore can produce good works in Him.

Can you see that our will, is now empowered to fight the good fight of faith? We can serve by exercising good deeds in the newness of our spirit, and put sin to death by the power of the Spirit.[290] An unbeliever is determined by his flesh whereas children of God are merely influenced by our flesh.[291] While we work, He gets the glory as His grace is the empowering agent. As the apostle wrote, "But by the grace of God I am what I am, and His grace toward me was not in vain; but I labored more abundantly than they all, yet not I, but the grace of God which was with me" (1 Corinthians 15:10).

With an understanding of how to fight, my prayer is summed up in a few verses of this song from Lex De Azevedo:

> The rain has set out to drown me right from the start
> Raging storms have delayed me, clouds have shaded my
>   heart
> But the sun has reflected my faith in its rays
> Smiling down as I follow His ways

---

[290] Romans 7:6, 8:13

[291] I owe this thought to Paul Maykish when we studied Romans 6 together.

Help me fight a good fight
Help me win with Thy might
Help me follow the Light
Help me Lord to fight a good fight[292]

---

[292] Music by Lex De Azevedo from the Saul of Tarsus movie from The Nest *Animated Stories of the New Testament.*

Testimony – Marked by His Love

Nyo Taji became addicted to alcohol and glue when he was seven years old. Before he could even read full sentences, he found himself in deep bondage to substance abuse. For eleven years, Nyo wrestled with depression, suicidal ideations, and anger.

In the early 2000s, if you were to visit Huruma Village or other surrounding slums, you would notice the rampant substance addictions that claimed the majority of the young men. Hundreds would wake up each morning without any sense of purpose and lie around the streets with a bottle of alcohol in their hands. When I visited Huruma in 2011, the sight of alcoholism was nearly gone. What changed?

The only way to cure an addiction is to replace it. If a person finds complete satisfaction, happiness, and pleasure in alcohol (or sex, money, fame…etc.), then he will continue to become a flesh-driven idolater. In order to be free, we have to let go of our idols and pursue the One who calls us to not be "drunk with wine, in which is dissipation; but be filled with the Spirit" (Ephesians 5:18). We can't just run *from* sin, we have to run *to* God.

Nyo came to the realization that Jesus was the only substance he needed to sustain his life. Over time, Jesus renewed his mind, gave him new desires, and freed him from the bondage of slavery to alcohol and other substances. Nyo's "god" of alcohol was replaced by God Himself. If you talk to Nyo today, he will tell you that God's grace saved him and he is now marked by His eternal love.

Questions for Reflection

1. How do you move your head knowledge to your heart?

2. How do you bear good fruit? Why is it important to inspect the fruit in our lives and others?

3. How does love connect to faith?

4. Is there someone in your life that you are failing to love? Why? What action steps are you going to take to change?

Verses to Memorize

2 Timothy 4:7
Romans 8:1-8, 13
1 Corinthians 15:10

CHAPTER 9

Knowing Jesus

But let him who glories glory in this, that he understands and knows Me, that I am the Lord, exercising lovingkindness, judgment, and righteousness in the earth. For in these I delight," says the LORD.

—Jeremiah 9:24

A little knowledge of God is worth more than a great deal of knowledge about Him.

—J.I. Packard

Knowing about isn't Knowing

When we observe Scripture, we discover that everyone in the world knows *about* God. It is true that atheists and some others claim to not believe that there is a God. But they are denying the obvious examples of God's fingerprints in nature and in the changed hearts of men and women. Their denial is not rational. At the same time, we see that those who are not children of God do not know Him. I understand that you may need to read that statement again. In other words, a person can know *about* God without actually knowing Him.

Paul informs three different churches (in Corinth, Galatia, and Thessalonica) that some people do not know God as a means for the salvation of their souls. They know *of Him*, but do not know Him as their personal Lord and Savior.

> "For since, in the wisdom of God, the world through wisdom did not know God, it pleased God through the foolishness of the message preached to save those who believe" (1 Corinthians 1:21).

> "But then, indeed, when you did not know God, you served those which by nature are not gods" (Galatians 4:8).

Those who are not children of God do not know Him and His glorious being and therefore cannot control their sinful passions, such as lust or greed.[293] They are slaves to their sin. Believers, on the other hand, are slaves to righteousness:[294] "And having become set free [from your sin], you became slaves of righteousness" (Romans 6:18).

Conversely, everyone in the world knows of God, even those who deny His existence. While slaves to sin, they suppress the truth of God. In order to suppress it, they would have to know about it. Paul discusses this in Romans 1:18-21 when he writes, that unbelievers "suppress the truth in unrighteousness, because what may be known of God is manifest in them…for since the creation of the world His invisible attributes are clearly seen, being understood by the things that are made…so that they are without excuse, because, although they knew God, they did not glorify Him as God, nor were thankful." Paul is clear that what can be known about God is visibly plain to all of us because He has revealed Himself to His entire creation. With this knowledge of God we are without excuse, and so at the Day of Judgment, those who have rejected Jesus will be condemned not because they "never heard the truth" but because

---

[293] 1 Thessalonians 4:4-5

[294] As my brother Michael says, "You are now a slave to freedom." Check out his website for gospel centered hip-hop style music www.betesbeats.weebly.com.

they suppressed the truth—exchanged God's glory for His creation.

We are all designed by God Himself with the capacity to know Him. However, in our willingness to sin, we try to substitute God for His creation and thus, commit idolatry. This space or void in our lives can never be satisfied unless God fills it with Himself. Only by the mercy and grace of God do we have the opportunity to allow Him (through His Son and by His Spirit) to fill the gap with the saving knowledge of the gospel. John Calvin said that the simple or mere knowledge of God, "can no more connect man with God, then the sight of the sun [can] carry him up to heaven."[295]

An Intimate Relationship

As her husband, I know my wife more intimately than any other person. It's a part of God's design for marriage that the two (man and woman) are to become one.[296] I know my wife better than anyone else in the world. Astonishingly, this intimate knowledge is actually analogous to our relationship with Jesus as portrayed in Scripture.

God said through the prophet Jeremiah that our

---

[295] John Calvin *The Problem of Pain*, 1940
[296] See Genesis 2:24-25

boasting in our wisdom, strength, or riches is futile. As a follower of Jesus Christ, the only thing we can boast in, is our understanding and knowledge of Him. Therefore, knowing Him is our delight in life.[297] The word 'know' is *yâda* in the Hebrew language and means an intimate knowledge of something or someone. The first time *yâda* is used in the Bible is in Genesis where we read, "Now Adam knew Eve his wife, and she conceived" (Genesis 4:1). Do you see that? Our desire to know God is more than a surface knowledge of Him.

In the New Testament, the Greek word for 'know' is *ginōskō*. Similar to *yâda*, this word was also a Jewish idiom for sexual intercourse between a man and a woman. Jesus said that He knows His children (sheep) by name, and they follow Him because they know His voice.[298] Those who know Him have life[299] and are safely secured in His eternal presence.

Furthermore, Jesus affirms the eternal importance of knowing Him as His words are recorded in Matthew's gospel. Jesus tells people to enter the narrow gate which leads to eternal life. We do this by knowing Him. After their physical death, many will say, *Lord, we have done good things. We have lived*

[297] Jeremiah 9:23-25
[298] See John 10:1-18
[299] John 10:10

a good life. We have followed your commands.[300] Jesus
will respond to those who think they can earn their
way into heaven with, "I never knew you; depart
from Me" (Matthew 7:23). We have to know Him.
If we don't, we will be eternally separated from Him.
God must also know us through our relationship
with Him.

> "And this is eternal life, that they may know You, the only
> true God, and Jesus Christ whom You have sent" (John
> 17:3).

How We Live

I asked a young man from Huruma Village how
he could live his life in peace while experiencing a
plethora of daily hardships. He responded with, "I am
at peace because I know Jesus Christ. And because I
know Him, I can follow and trust Him." You see my
friend, knowing Jesus changes how we think and live.
When we love God, we are known by Him. When
we love Him, we walk in His ways.[301]

This young man's life was characterized by His
relationship with Jesus. His circumstances became
irrelevant because his hope in the Lord dictated his
life. Obeying God's commands was not burdensome,

[300] See Matthew 7:21-23
[301] See 1 Corinthians 8:2-3

as he expressed his love for the Creator of all good things.[302]

Know Him by Listening to Him

Paul warned us that in the last days leading up to Christ's return, many people will seek and find teachers that tell them what they want to hear.

> "For the time will come when they will not endure sound doctrine, but according to their own desires, because they have itching ears, they will heap up for themselves teachers; and they will turn their ears away from the truth, and be turned aside to fables" (2 Timothy 4:3-4).

Sadly, more and more people (even in the church) will squash any desire to read the Bible and turn to these teachers who affirm or validate their personal, and unbiblical desires.

This is why there are so many verses that are twisted out of context to "fit" with or approve the sin in the culture. What would happen if everyone in our churches, small groups, Bible studies, and families had a real desire to be devoted to the study of Scripture?[303] I believe we will gain understanding, wisdom, and discernment as we spend time listening

---

[302] See 1 John 5:1-5; James 1:17

[303] Acts 2:42 describes the early Christian's devotion in foundational Christian disciplines.

to Jesus who is the Truth.[304] This truth is found in His Word.[305] We get to know Him by listening to Him!

When We Know Jesus, We Follow Him

Jesus is the image of the invisible God.[306] The word for image in the Greek is *eikōn*. The meaning of the word is a derivation of someone or something. Derivation is different from imitation.

This distinction in Scripture is essential because of how the English language translates the Greek word *mimētēs*. Paul uses this word when he tells the Corinthian church, "Imitate me, just as I also imitate Christ" (1 Corinthians 11:1). He also instructs the church in Ephesus to be, "imitators of God as dear children" (Ephesians 5:1). The Greek word used here does not mean *copy* but rather to *follow*.

This is what God desires of His children. He wants them to follow Him. My children copy me all the time. If I ask my daughter to pick up her toys, and she repeats or imitates my command verbally, what good does that do? I want her to follow me. I want her to follow my example as I imperfectly follow Jesus.

---

[304] John 14:6
[305] John 17:17
[306] Colossians 1:15

Only in Christ do I have any light to offer to others. When we know Jesus, we follow Him.

A brother of mine once told me that a man's worth is shown in how much of God is reflected in his life. So we have to ask ourselves, "Do we follow God?" We follow God because Jesus gave His life *for* us (blood transaction at the cross) so that He could give His life *to* us (blood transfusion at Pentecost). In other words, God *laid down* His life so that we could *receive* His life in our new birth.

Listen to some of the words from Graham Kendrick as he penned a song of the joy of knowing Jesus in *Knowing You*.

> All I once held dear, built my life upon
> All this world reveres, and wars to own
> All I once thought gain I have counted loss
> Spent and worthless now, compared to this
>
> Knowing you, Jesus
> Knowing you, there is no greater thing
> You're my all, you're the best
> You're my joy, my righteousness[307]

---

[307] Kendrick, Graham. *Knowing You*. Make Way Music. 1993.

Testimony – Radiant

> "For My thoughts are not your thoughts,
> Nor are your ways My ways," says the Lord.
> "For as the heavens are higher than the earth,
> So are My ways higher than your ways,
> And My thoughts than your thoughts" (Isaiah 55:8-9).

Subira Maina died from a preventable disease not too long after I visited her home. Her countenance magnified her internal smile, as she described the hardships she experienced growing up as an abandoned orphan in an African slum. Like all of us, she was made in His image (see Genesis 1:27). As a Christian, she reflected Jesus' image by rejoicing in her suffering.

God bids us to pray. But we have to acknowledge that His ways are not our ways. The concept of God's sovereign will proves difficult to understand when we attempt to answer life's questions on our own. The apostle Paul says that God's will is good, pleasing, and perfect. Really? Perfect? How is His will perfect when he allows suffering to take place in the world? In a moment of suffering, goodness seems absent. But, as Christians, we claim God's promises that *all* things work together for our good and His glory (see Romans 8).

"And not only that, but we also glory in tribulations, knowing that tribulation produces perseverance; and perseverance, character; and character, hope. Now hope does not disappoint, because the love of God has been poured out in our hearts by the Holy Spirit who was given to us" (Romans 5:3-5).

Questions for Reflection

1. Do you know Jesus or just know about Him? What is the difference?

2. In your own words, what does it mean to know Jesus?

3. What is the difference between loving The Bible and loving its Author?

4. Do you copy Jesus or follow Him? How do you know?

Verses to Memorize

Jeremiah 9:23-24
John 10:14-15
John 17:3

CHAPTER 10

What is the Gospel?

For all have sinned and fall short of the glory of God, being justified freely by His grace through the redemption that is in Christ Jesus, whom God set forth as a propitiation by His blood, through faith, to demonstrate His righteousness, because in His forbearance God had passed over the sins that were previously committed, to demonstrate at the present time His righteousness, that He might be just and the justifier of the one who has faith in Jesus.

—Romans 3:23-36

The gospel is not a doctrine of the tongue, but of life. It cannot be grasped by reason and memory only, but it is fully understood when it possesses the whole soul and penetrates to the inner recesses of the heart.

—John Calvin

A Great Exchange

I entitled the first chapter "What is Suffering?" for a specific reason. The more you analyze suffering in your life, the more you will see the need for a true Savior. Life is messy. Hardships are guaranteed. We turn on the television and constantly hear bad news. Pain, sickness, and death overwhelm the headlines. We deeply long for good news. This is where the gospel gives us genuine hope. Without the gospel, life is meaningless.

The gospel is the good news that the one and only true God, the gracious and just Creator of the world, has looked upon hopelessly sinful men and women and sent His son, Jesus Christ, God in the flesh. Jesus was sent to bear the Father's wrath against sin through His substitutionary death on the cross, and to show His power over sin and death in the resurrection from the grave. All who deny themselves and turn from their sin, and trust in Jesus alone as Lord and Savior of their lives, will be reconciled to God forever.[308]

Every human being by their nature and choice is born with a void in their lives. This void will never be satisfied unless Jesus Christ Himself, fills it. When suffering strikes—whether poverty or pain,

---

[308] See Romans 3:21-26

we find it easy to blame God and think, *If He exists, He would never allow such terrible things to happen.* Without an understanding and knowledge of God's unfathomable love, we cannot begin to make sense of our daily hardships.

Consider what God has done as He lovingly sacrificed His Son on the cross for our sins. Not one of us would even consider laying down our life for those who hate us. And yet, although we never asked for Him to sacrificially die for our sins, and certainly didn't deserve this sacrificial love, "while we were still sinners, Christ died for us" (Romans 5:8).

All of us, by our nature and choice, sin.[309] Our willing rebellion separates us from the Holy God of this universe.[310] In contrast, Jesus knew no sin.[311] In a great exchange, Jesus took our place. He lived the life we could never live and died the death we could never die by laying down His life on the cross, and taking our place. So what do we need to do?

Repent

Repentance requires genuine humility, a rare character trait. *Build yourself up. Get ahead in life.*

---

[309] Romans 3:23

[310] Romans 6:23; 1 Corinthians 6:9-10; Hebrews 1:13

[311] 2 Corinthians 5:21

Only the strongest survive. These phrases in our culture lead us toward a heart filled with pride. This pride is destructive and keeps us from understanding the truth of our depravity apart from God.

The Greek word for "repent" in the New Testament is *metanoeō* which means to think differently, and to change course. We are to repent of our sins by hating them and running from them toward Jesus. There is a difference though, between worldly repentance and godly repentance. A person may repent or feel sorry for a sin in their life and even stop committing the sin, but this is just a result of repenting, not repentance itself. It is true that repentance will result in a change of our actions.[312] However, when God calls us to repentance, He means for us to acknowledge our sins, confess them, and know that we cannot save ourselves or get on good terms by our own works.

Another way to understand repentance is to change our mind in regard to Jesus Christ. In Peter's sermon on Pentecost, he calls the people who have rejected Jesus to repent. He is calling them to change their minds and surrender to Jesus as the "Lord and Savior" (Acts 2:36). All of us are alienated from God because of our sin, wanting to be our own God. By God's grace, we have to change our mind from rejection of Christ to faith in Him. In order to run

---

[312] See Matthew 3:8; Luke 3:13-14; Acts 3:19, 26:20

toward Jesus with true repentance, we have to believe in Him.

Believe

Apart from repentance, belief is void. "Even the demons believe [in the existence of Jesus]—and tremble" (James 2:19)! I believe in a lot of things. I believe that the chair I am sitting in is strong enough to hold me. My belief pushes me to have faith. This faith is acted out by sitting in the chair itself.

Everyone believes in the existence of God, even atheists if they were totally honest, and even the demons though they have rejected Him.[313] God has made us in His image with a conscience to know right and wrong. He has further manifested His divine existence by showing His glorious creation that surrounds us.[314] Our belief is a matter of trust. Do we trust Him—the Truth?

The question is: what do you believe about Jesus? This is what separates all other faiths or world religions. Do you believe in Jesus for who He is, or have you made up a false Jesus to justify the way you live your life?

Scripture is clear as Jesus clearly stated that He is

---

[313] James 2:19
[314] See Romans 1:20-21

God who became flesh, and dwelt among mankind without losing His deity.[315] Because of His deity, Jesus was able to pay for our sins by dying on the cross and overcoming death by resurrecting three days later. The historical evidence of Jesus' life, crucifixion, and resurrection is unquestionable.[316]

Worship

We were created to do two things: worship God and rule over His creation in His Name. Instead, we rebelled against God and separated ourselves from Him. The original created order was turned upside down when Adam and Eve rejected God.

All of us try to fill the void of God in our hearts and are driven to idolatry to fill that void. An idol in our life is anything or anyone that we worship or prefer rather than God Himself. By our nature and choice, we worship creation instead of the Creator.[317] As a result, we are ruled by what we worship.

We can identify idols in our life by asking some basic, yet revealing questions. What does your heart wander to? What preoccupies the majority of your time? What do you do in your solitude? What do

---

[315] John 10:30, 1:14

[316] I encourage you to read Lee Strobel's books: *The Case for Christ* and *The Case for the Resurrection*.

[317] Romans 1:25

you use to comfort yourself when things go wrong? What do you worry about the most? How do you "medicate" the pain in your life? What stirs your affections? Where do you find hope and satisfaction?

Some idols are easy to identify: money, sex, work, material possessions, relationships...etc. Others are like deep waters, and it takes a person of wisdom and understanding to draw them out.[318]

Maybe you idolize *consent* (i.e. *approval*)—you only feel good when you are loved and respected by a certain individual or a social group. You chase after praise and recognition from others. You find more joy at work where you are applauded for your success, then at home where you have to constantly die to yourself and serve others. When a person idolizes approval, he or she may spend long hours at work in order to avoid responsibility and difficulty at home— i.e. reality. Success in a vocation is usually easier to achieve than success as a spouse or parent.

Maybe you idolize *comfort*—you need a certain quality of life that has a lack of stress and an abundance of freedom without any trials or hardships. You may idolize comfort and become a workaholic maintain a comfortable lifestyle or standard of living. This standard of living will continue to become more extravagant as you "climb the corporate ladder." You

---

[318] Proverbs 20:5

worry that if you don't work hard to "get ahead" financially, socially, or vocationally, your family will be forced to live an uncomfortable lifestyle. You live to work rather than work to live. Do you see the difference?

Maybe you idolize *control*—you only feel like you have worth if you gain absolute certainty in your life. You may work hard in your vocation, but your motive is to control your life or your future. You struggle to let others help you with your tasks because only you can "get it done right and on time." You feel overwhelmed when others have responsibility that directly affects your quality of life or career.

Or perhaps you idolize *command* (i.e. *power)*—you seek to gain influence and achieve success. Your motive for diligent work is really from deep in your heart to chase after bigger promotions and more (or seemingly more) responsibility. Without success, your life seems meaningless. Many parents can attest that our competitive sports culture breeds this particular idol extremely well.

How do you kill the idols in your life? First, repent and then turn from them and find your ultimate joy in Christ. Embrace the truth of the gospel. Transfer your trust from your idols to the Savior. Let Jesus become your ultimate joy. See Jesus for who He is. He is more valuable, offers more hope, and is more desirable than anything or anyone. Jesus must become the chief affection of your heart—your inner self. Ultimately, in order to remove these idols in your life, you have to believe the gospel of Jesus Christ.

The gospel is the good news that in His life by His death, and with His resurrection, Jesus Christ secured for us all the affection, achievement, control, comfort, command, meaning, purpose, and protection that we deeply desire every day. In other words, Jesus Christ became our Savior. He replaced our idols. He gave us Himself—the only One who is worthy of our worship!

The truth of Jesus and the gift of salvation are easy to find, but hard to accept. Where are you on this journey? Are you ready for a new dawn? Are you ready for a new life in Jesus Christ?

Testimony – Forever Changed

It is often said that Jesus plus nothing equals everything. While visiting Huruma village, God showed me a group of people who worshiped Him with all their hearts. From ashes to beauty, the villagers understood why they can rejoice in the midst of suffering.

Since last visiting my brothers and sisters of Huruma, I've struggled to try and comprehend the complexities of the human heart. Indeed, my life has been forever changed. While Mji wa Huruma Village was once known as the pit from which no one can escape, I believe God has shown this group of people that they cannot escape His love. In a beautiful way that brings glory to God, many of them have discovered that Jesus minus everything is still everything.

My dear friend, do you know Jesus?

Questions for Reflection

1. Who is Jesus to you? Is your understanding of Him based on the truth found in His Word?

2. Have you repented and believed in Jesus Christ as your Lord and Savior?

3. If you are a child of God, write down three things that you will do to demonstrate your faith.

Verses to Memorize

Romans 3:23
Romans 5:3-10
Romans 10:9-10

ABOUT THE AUTHOR

❖❖❖

Charles Prichard is a husband, father, teacher, mentor, and an officer in the United States Air Force (USAF). He feels passionate about teaching the importance of a biblical worldview and how we can mentor, teach, and encourage others to apply God's Word to everyday life. He prays that people will find themselves both encouraged and edified by his book, as they seek God in the midst of the hardships of life.

Charles holds a BA in Systems Engineering Management from the USAF Academy and a MA in Human Services Counseling, specifically, Military Resilience from Liberty University. He is also a MS in Project Management candidate at the University of Texas at Dallas.

Charles and his beautiful wife, Whitney, are enjoying their growing family and currently reside in Texas.

I would love to hear your story as it pertains to this book. My contact information is below so feel free to ask questions, critique, comment, or just say hujambo! Thank you for reading.

Facebook: facebook.com/prichardministries

Twitter: t w i t t e r . c o m / P r i c h a r d C h a r l e s
@Prichard Charles

YouTube: youtube.com/channel   UCFvwg
BD8ubvJ x4USkXHeiA
Search for Charles J. Prichard or Prichard Ministries.

Blog: prichardspassus.wordpress.com

Prichard Ministries seeks to spread the gospel of Jesus Christ around the world through books, conferences, & other venues. Psalm 71:18 is our prayer!

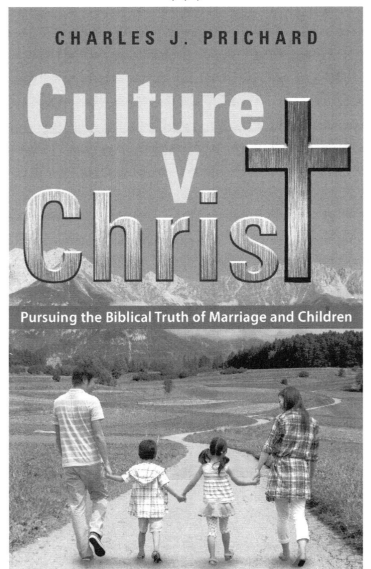

CHARLES J. PRICHARD

Culture
v.
Christ

Pursuing the Biblical Truth of Marriage and Children

CULTURE V. CHRIST: PURSUING THE BIBLICAL TRUTH OF MARRIAGE AND CHILDREN

❖❖❖

What has happened to the American Christian church? Divorce rates are skyrocketing, children are not being raised to fear God and follow His commands, and families are being ripped apart.

The truth is that all areas of our life get twisted when we stray from the perfect guidance and laws of the Word of God. When we avoid looking at these important life subjects through the lens of the gospel, we fall flat on our face. As a society, we have developed so many different nuances that contradict God's Word. There are many people in the church who have looked to culture and have conformed to the godless patterns of this world. Why do we so easily fall into the temptation to justify our sins and excuse our shortcomings?

Is it possible that many born-again Christians are missing the mark more often than they think? Many who do not have a biblical understanding on how they should live, raise a family, or cultivate a marriage. Many who wander through life casually and turn to